Collectable Names and Designs in Women's Handbags

Hermès custom shiny *Rose Scheherazade* crocodile & *Vert Vertigo* alligator *Constance 24* bag with permabrass hardware. Sold at Christie's Hong Kong, 2018 for $7,500.

Collectable Names and Designs in Women's Handbags

Tracy Martin

With A Foreword

By

Sarah Delves

PEN & SWORD
HISTORY

First published in Great Britain in 2021 by
Pen & Sword History
An imprint of
Pen & Sword Books Ltd
Yorkshire – Philadelphia

ISBN 978 1 78159 745 3

Typeset by Mac Style
Printed and bound in India by Replika Press Pvt Ltd.

Pen & Sword Books Limited incorporates the imprints of Atlas, Archaeology,
Aviation, Discovery, Family History, Fiction, History, Maritime, Military,
Military Classics, Politics, Select, Transport, True Crime, Air World, Frontline
Publishing, Leo Cooper, Remember When, Seaforth Publishing, The Praetorian
Press, Wharncliffe Local History, Wharncliffe Transport, Wharncliffe True
Crime and White Owl.

For a complete list of Pen & Sword titles please contact

PEN & SWORD BOOKS LIMITED
47 Church Street, Barnsley, South Yorkshire, S70 2AS, England
E-mail: enquiries@pen-and-sword.co.uk
Website: www.pen-and-sword.co.uk

Or

PEN AND SWORD BOOKS
1950 Lawrence Rd, Havertown, PA 19083, USA
E-mail: Uspen-and-sword@casematepublishers.com
Website: www.penandswordbooks.com

Dedication

For my mum who cannot resist buying yet another handbag even though she has far too many already! And never stops me from buying another for my collection either!

Contents

Foreword

When I was a child handbags and purses held little or no interest for me. I loved ballet and dance and was fascinated by things that sparkled but I also enjoyed getting muddy, climbing trees and riding my bike.

It wasn't until I reached my late teens and early twenties that my love of handbags began to develop. It came from nowhere, there was no influence from my mother or either of my grandmothers. Although they carried handbags they were not particular fans of bags, so there was little or no encouragement from them. I was never really that fashion-conscious but where bags were concerned I was in my element. They could express something that, perhaps, at that time, I couldn't.

Although I have been in the antiques and collectables trade since the early 1990s, handbags and accessories didn't feature until around 2004 when I was watching a well-known antiques programme and saw something that not only sparked my curiosity but was the start of a complete change in direction for me career-wise and saw the beginning of my business, Bags of Glamour. The bags in question were Lucite purses and from the moment I saw them I was hooked! It wasn't just that they were the most incredible bags I had ever seen, it was the fantastic designs, many reflecting the art-deco style. They were incredibly glamorous and it was a material I had never heard of before.

And so it began: the buying, the researching, the learning, making many mistakes but most of all thoroughly enjoying every minute and developing a specialist knowledge that has brought me a wealth of opportunities.

Today I am lucky enough to buy and sell the most glorious and unusual antique and vintage handbags from circa 1750 to the present day, with a special interest in Lucite. I lecture on my subject across the United Kingdom and exhibit at some of the best antiques fairs in the country, as well as doing occasional auction consultancy work in vintage and designer handbag sales.

Handbags can be so many things. A functional item to cart around your necessary bits and pieces, a fashion statement, an extension of your personality or an investment for the future. They can be whatever you want them to be.

I was absolutely delighted and honoured to be asked by Tracy to write the foreword for her book *Collectable Names and Designs in Women's Handbags* as I share her love of handbags, her passion for the unusual, the quirky and most importantly the fun!

Tracy loves and understands handbags and this book examines so many aspects, including a look into handbag history, their social relevance, the stratospheric rise in the desirability of the designer bag, tips on what to look for and a look into the collectors' pieces of the future.

Tracy has inspired so many people with her love of fashion and accessories, which, coupled with her fun and engaging personality and specialist knowledge, means this book will be a must-have for anyone with an interest in handbags and their history as her passion for handbags of all eras shines through and transports you into handbag heaven.

I know that as you read *Collectable Names and Designs in Women's Handbags* you too will fall in love with the carefully picked and researched handbags that Tracy has chosen. Tracy shares her expert knowledge and enthusiasm for history, innovation, creativity and design and this blends seamlessly with her obvious love of the handbags. I know that this passion and enthusiasm cannot fail to inspire and delight you.

Sarah Delves, founder of Bags of Glamour

Sarah Delves.

Introduction

*I*adore handbags! The reason being that no matter your age, body shape or origin, bags are one of the main fashion accessories that you can choose without having to worry about any of the above. You simply choose a bag to suit your needs or, in my case, to reflect personality rather than practicality. Handbags for me need to be fun, quirky and extroverted – basically the more novel the better. I love embellishment, unusual designs and stand-out bags that scream 'this is a woman that loves to be different'. Don't get me wrong, I appreciate the classic and simple designs but personally prefer my arm candy to make a statement and mirror who I am as a person.

So when I was asked to write this book, *Collectable Names & Designs in Women's Handbags*, I found myself transported to handbag heaven. Spending my days looking at images of remarkable bags, indulging myself in researching information on the history of the handbag, together with learning the fascinating stories behind the innovative designers and where they gained their inspiration.

I have also explored the social history of our handbag heritage as this has played a huge part in the progression of bag design. Over the decades, new materials or machinery have allowed manufacturers to break new ground, enabling them to experiment with their designs. In this book I will look at how each decade impacted on the humble handbag, with certain events or moments in time contributing to the advancement of this fashion accessory. Some designs epitomise an era, evoke nostalgic memories or reflect the music, film or social scenes of a particular decade. Recognised as important fashion artefacts, many are now housed in museums all around the world, on display so that people can appreciate that handbags through the ages are very much part of our social history and heritage. A fascinating trip through the evolution of the handbag, this has been one of the areas I have found most interesting and in turn, it has made me appreciate why the bag has become one of the most important fashion statements of our time.

The book also, as the title suggests, focuses on the collectability of handbags, so in my job as a fashion collectables expert, I will explain and consider why bags have become so desirable in collectors' circles and in some cases, the extortionate amount of money that collectors are willing to pay for the very best designer examples. I will be sharing my knowledge on what to look out for, along with giving tips on where to buy and how not to get scammed by fakes. I will be suggesting which handbags I feel are worth investing in, both as a collector's piece and as that must-have fashion accessory. For example, the vintage mesh bags dating from the 1920s and 1930s, the Lucite of the 1950s, and the bag that first made an appearance in the 1980s and has since become the 'holy grail' that is the Hermès *Birkin*.

I will also be looking at twenty-first century handbags as collectors' pieces by showcasing modern designers whose talents are displayed in eye-catching, innovative handbag designs at more affordable prices, and advising on which ones to snap up

Irregular Choice *Amore* bag with large laser-cut acrylic love heart embellishment on a glitter rainbow and stars background.

as collectables of the future. These bags are constantly pushing the boundaries as designers not only strive to innovate but also recognise that the handbag market is growing, with women wanting increasingly elaborate and breathtaking designs.

The fabrication of handbags has reached new heights. Now, they can be classed as works of art that would happily grace any gallery installation. Innovative, sculptural and decorative, in today's modern society handbags are far from simply practical vessels for carrying around essentials. Instead, they are recognised for their artistic merit. This book will also pay homage to the talented designers that take the basic form of a bag and create a mini-masterpiece, elegantly displayed on the arms of women that appreciate fashion as an art form.

A book written with a love for the subject, I guarantee that as you read *Collectable Names & Designs in Women's Handbags* you will start to look at handbags with fresh eyes, as you wonder at the designs and learn from the history. It's packed full of images of extraordinary, innovative and desirable handbags (and even a few famous ones), along with in-depth information on the progression of handbag design and the gifted designers who create them. This book is a celebration of a practical yet fascinating fashion accessory and I know that as you turn the pages, you too will find yourself transported into handbag heaven!

Chapter 1

Collecting Handbags

'When it comes to bags, men, and cities, is it really what's outside that counts?'

Carrie Bradshaw, Sex and the City

Carrie Bradshaw hit the nail on the head, as I believe that no truer words have ever been spoken about bags (well, possibly men and cities, too, but I am more concerned with bags). For me, it is what's displayed on the outside of the handbag that first grabs my attention and starts my heart racing. I seek out the extraordinary and hunt for the unusual, whether that be a vintage example or a bang up-to-date modern bag. They have to speak to me, and as soon as they do I am instantly drawn in. Between this and my insatiable passion for handbag fashion, I now own quite an eclectic collection.

When it comes to the serious business of collecting handbags there are many paths you can choose to go down. Some prefer to acquire early antique bags pre-dating the nineteenth century but this is difficult, as few are available to the modern collector. More common are collectors of bags dating from the mid-nineteenth century onwards. There is particular interest in twentieth-century bags, as there is a huge selection to choose from and they are much easier to source. Many dedicate their collection to one particular decade or concentrate on a specific style, such as 1920s beaded bags or American 1950s Lucite bags. In recent years, though, more and more collectors have realised the importance of modern handbags, especially within the luxury handbag industry. Today, there is great demand on the secondary market, as collectors look to auctions to acquire those must-own luxury designer handbags. These bags now fetch exorbitant prices when they turn up for sale, such as the featured Hermès custom shiny *Rose Scheherazade* crocodile & *Vert Vertigo* alligator *Constance 24* with permabrass hardware, pictured earlier, which sold at Christie's Hong Kong in 2018 for $7,500.

This elaborately embroidered purse probably corresponds to the 'sweet bags' recorded in a number of sixteenth- and seventeenth-century inventories. These purses appear to have been worn about the person and carried scented herbs and essences to ward off the evil smells of daily life.

Regardless of the avenue you choose to explore, the main point of collecting any fashion item is that you buy it because you love it. Bags are meant to be used and meant to be seen, so the golden rule is that you gain enjoyment from the bags and feel proud as you walk down the street with your newest acquisition swinging from your shoulder or perched proudly on your arm.

Equally important to note is that handbag collecting should be fun. Choose bags that you are instantly attracted to. These could be bags by a certain designer or of a particular style, perhaps even vintage bags that are made of a specific material. You could also consider, like me, collecting a diverse range of handbags that suit your own personal taste.

I personally have a varied collection with a plethora of colours and designs. Some are for daytime, others reserved for evening. Many are fun fashion bags with glitzy embellishment, while some are classic designer. I love nothing more than someone exclaiming 'I love your bag!' and this is a remark I hear often as I walk down the street or dance the night away in a bar. My only slight problem is that I do not always buy with my practical head on and often find that the bag I have taken on a night out looks amazing but doesn't hold all of my essentials.

Whatever aspect of handbag collecting you decide to explore, I guarantee that you will have your eyes opened wide as you enter a world of wonder, becoming handbag obsessed. Wanting them all, needing them all! This infectious addiction will turn you into a handbag-o-holic, as you are embroiled in the amazing designs available to you, and I promise it won't be long before you find you have amassed a very impressive collection.

Collecting antique bags

As already mentioned, collecting very early handbags from before the nineteenth century is difficult as most are housed in museums. This elaborately embroidered seventeenth-century British purse, for example, resides in the Met Museum in New York. These purses were typically worn about the person

A reticule is a type of women's drawstring handbag, made of beading or brocade and used in the eighteenth and nineteenth century.

and carried scented herbs and essences to ward off the evil smells of daily life. On the rare occasion that an early example does come up for sale, collectors and museums compete against each other to win these scarce examples. So, a good place to start your collection is with bags dating from the nineteenth century onwards.

There are a variety of options open to collectors of nineteenth-century bags. Miser purses (otherwise known as string, finger or ring purses) often come up for sale, as do dainty embroidered and beaded examples, along with chatelaine bags designed to be worn suspended from the waist of a skirt

Victorian women needed purses for social engagements to carry their calling cards, pencils and handkerchief.

Nineteenth-century miser purse in dark blue decorated with cut steel, having steel tassel decoration. Gifted to Brooklyn Museum Costume Collection, The Metropolitan Museum of Art by Mr and Mrs Maxine L. Hermanos.

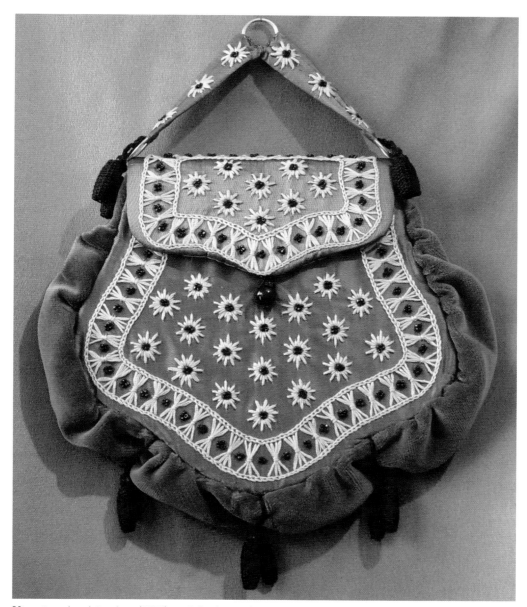

Victorian chatelaine bag (1875) with buckram frame, covered in embroidered silk taffeta. Tiny black glass pearls from a late Victorian mourning dress highlight the design. The outside is covered in velvet.

and dangled down the side of the hip. Carpet bags were also popular during the Victorian era as they were the perfect choice when something more substantial was needed for travelling. The perfect platform for a lady to show off her sewing skills, the large majority of bags during this period were homemade, and it is these needlework bags that are the easiest to find when out antique bag-hunting. They are also a great place to start, as many are very affordable.

The array of different styles and designs available to buyers of nineteenth-century bags are not only popular with avid collectors but also those who recognise the desirability of owning a bag of historical importance. Modern handbag designers look to original antique pieces for inspiration, as these early examples provide great insight into the heritage of handbag design.

The array of different styles and designs available to buyers of nineteenth-century bags are not only popular with avid collectors but also those who recognise the desirability of owning a bag of historical importance. Modern handbag designers look to original antique pieces for inspiration, as these early examples provide great insight into the heritage of handbag design.

Early twentieth-century handbag collecting

This is where handbag collecting gets really exciting as the bag starts to evolve, becoming evocative of its era. The metal mesh bags most notably made by both Whiting and Davis and the Mandalian Manufacturing Co. become hugely popular and are today keenly collected, as are the small metal purses originally worn around the neck. The Dorothy bag, again a popular accessory from the turn of the century, continues to be a favourite, and small embroidered and beaded bags are used. The vibrant Jazz Age of the 1920s brings an array of designs such as the envelope-shaped pochettes that are tucked under the arm and hand-tooled leather handbags similar to styles we use today. The 1930s bring more elaborately designed evening bags, while simple but stylish day bags ooze quiet sophistication. Handbags from these decades embody the femininity of the times and as you start to consider all forms of this accessory from these eras you will find yourself transported back in time, when every style-conscious woman wanted her bag to be an extension of her glamorous lifestyle.

'Ladies of the middle classes... in hansom carriages as they paid afternoon calls. Their white kid gloves were of immaculate quality. Over one wrist they carried a small, square, gold *mesh bag containing a gold pencil, a handkerchief, and a flat gold wallet which held their calling cards.'*

Cecil Beaton, photographer and designer, taken from The Glass of Fashion

Another great area of collecting is the 1940s. Practicality was paramount as women needed to carry around more necessities such as a coin purse, gloves, make-up, a mirror and sometimes a cigarette case. The bags of this period were larger shoulder bags, making them easier to carry, and the style was mainly utilitarian, so without rich embellishments. Homemade fabric bags were essential due to wartime shortages, as were knitted and crocheted handmade designs. Towards the end of the decade, bags did become more innovative, with box bags first making an appearance and fashion designers beginning to experiment with their designs. Again, there is an eclectic array of bags that can easily be picked up in vintage clothes shops or online through specialist handbag retailers at affordable prices, so personally I think this is a great place to start your twentieth-century vintage handbag collection.

Collect and invest in handbags that epitomise an era. Not only will you be holding history in your hands, you will instantly feel yourself transported back to another time when fashion was the order of the day.

The mid-century onwards

Wow! This is where vintage handbag collecting is at. The most desirable bags all date from the 1950s and beyond because there is a wealth of styles and designs to choose from. Fashion really turned a corner after the war and as a result, collectors recognise this as an important period in fashion history. There is so much on offer from the 1950s, from Lucite box bags to high-end designer handbags such as the Hermès *Kelly* and the Chanel *2.55*. The 1960s saw new materials innovatively used in bags, while 1970s design was inspired by the hippie scene and straw, patent and textured materials. In the 1980s, a decadent time for fashion, the flashier and more expensive the better; big designer names such as Gucci, Hermès, Louis Vuitton,

1950s clear Lucite Myles handbag featuring a carved lid embellished with multi-coloured crystals, with gold hardware and an original label.

Fendi and Chanel represented status and power. Metallic hues, chain mail and metal embellishment were prominent throughout the decade, while the clutch was another status symbol. Available in all sizes, it was seen tucked under the arms of glamorous celebrities and was seen to add a touch of elegance and class to any outfit.

If you are hunting out bags for investment, this is a period that must not be ignored. Some of the most iconic bags were born in the mid- to late-twentieth century and it is these particular handbags that are in high demand from collectors. Prices are constantly increasing at the luxury end of the market, but they have been on the rise for vintage bags across the board over the past decade or so. Collectors recognise the important role that the humble bag has played in our social history, and want to own a unique piece that will make the wearer stand out in a crowd. These innovative bags represent times gone by and as a result are now a buoyant market in collecting circles. Rightfully so, as twentieth-century vintage bags led the way in the development of the accessory.

When it comes to collecting and investing in high-end luxury handbags, both vintage and modern, it is best to buy from specialist auction houses or reputable dealers. Condition is paramount, so ensure that you check your purchase over properly before even considering buying, speak to the specialist, ask questions and see if there is any paperwork for proof that the bag is genuine, as there are many counterfeits on the market. Be similarly mindful of condition when looking for vintage examples that are evocative of their era, as these, like all vintage fashion items, have been used. Ensure there is no damage, such as cracks or splits in plastic bags, ink or make-up spillages on linings, and that any hardware is in good order. There are, however, many more reliable outlets when purchasing more affordable vintage bags. Visit fashion fairs, vintage clothes shops, online retailers and smaller general auction houses and handle the bags yourself to get a feel for what you are buying. This is the quickest way to learn – you're bound to make the odd mistake, as we all do, but this is how you eventually get to spot that prized possession.

Modern handbag collecting

I am a firm believer that when it comes to modern handbag collecting, the bags you buy today could very well increase in value quite rapidly; some might even end up displayed in museums in the future.

When I go handbag shopping, I tend to veer towards those that I feel have the potential to become future fashion collectables. I look for distinctive design, quirky styles and stand-out bags that instantly say 'buy me'. I like to think outside the box, looking at modern handbags through the eyes of a collector. Classic bags by renowned designers always stand the test of time, as do bags that have been created as part of a fashion collaboration. Look for bags that are released under licence through a designer or retail outlet and consider special limited edition bags that are only made in very small numbers. Bags such as the Yoshi *Ivy Boutique* (pictured) are definitely worth considering, as aside from being wonderfully fun and eye-catching, each are hand-finished with detailed appliqués, making them more interesting to a collector.

Classic designer bags will always have staying power, as often it is the name behind the bag as much as the bag itself that ensures desirability. This doesn't necessarily mean you have to remortgage your property to buy one, as there are many designers like Vivienne Westwood, Lulu Guinness and Moschino that produce stunning, stylish designer handbags at reasonable prices.

Themed bags are also really popular in collecting circles. Handbags displaying festive Christmas scenes or spooky Halloween decorations are keenly sought after, as are bags with Disney motifs.

Collect handbags that you believe have the potential to become design classics of the future.

Yoshi *Ivy Boutique* pink leather multiway grab bag.

Some people choose to amass a collection of animal-themed handbags, perhaps focusing on bags featuring cats or dogs, while others favour glitzy embellishment with as much sparkle as possible. Many collectors are inclined to purchase handbags that are simple yet stylish and steer clear of rich colours or embellishment. However,

Irregular Choice *Ghost House* Halloween limited edition bag.

I feel that if you want your collection to stand out then you need to inject some sense of fun into your arm candy. As mentioned previously, handbag collecting is very much down to personal taste and the designs that reflect your mood or personality, but if you are buying a bag as a future collectable then there needs to be something more adventurous about it, whether that be the outward design or the designer label attached.

Unfortunately, I do not have a crystal ball to tell me exactly which bags will become winners in the profit stakes and how much time must pass before they realise their price potential. I can, however, advise on how to have a keener eye and to buy wisely in the hope that your bags will become desirable collectables in the future.

Contemporary artistic merits

Today, many people appreciate the aesthetics of handbag design, meaning bags are now much more than just functional vessels for helping us to carry our essentials – they can be works of art in their own right. Collectors often proudly display their collections in glass-fronted cabinets, while Singapore socialite Jamie Chua has a secure fingerprint-protected walk-in wardrobe to house her vast collection of Hermès bags.

Singapore socialite Jamie Chua is thought to have the world's largest Hermès *Birkin* collection, numbering over 200 bags.

Innovation in handbag design can be found all over the retail market. You only have to step inside the large London department stores to see the array of eye-catching handbags enticing those that appreciate their artistic merits. Each and every high-end concession showcases the exceptional talents of the designers when it comes to creating jaw-dropping bags, blowing shoppers away with bejewelled treasures, novelty themes, sophisticated embroidery and remarkable workmanship.

It is not just the luxury manufacturers that realise the full potential of the handbag and its commercial demand; astounding creations can be found from more affordable brands, too. Irregular Choice are renowned for their exceptional shoe designs but also produce breathtaking handbags, and companies such as Skinnydip have caught on to the power of the novelty handbag, with their amazing cross-body designs amassing a great following among devotees of the distinctive.

Nowadays, there is no end to the possibilities when it comes to creating visually captivating works in handbag form. Freedom of artistic expression has reached new levels, with designers able to realise their visions in countless possible permutations. The bodies and handles of bags can be made from a variety of different materials, clasp and hardware designs can be constantly innovated, the shape can be changed and the outer design can capture anything the designer wishes. Inspiration is drawn from a variety of mediums, traditions and historical influences. Some designs embrace the out-there and the over-the-top, while others embody a more classic style. Large shoulder bags, small evening bags, cross-bodies, totes, backpacks and clutches – there is a bag for every need, occasion and taste. The most difficult decision is which one to choose, as all have their unique selling points.

This is true when it comes to buying vintage bags as well. The bags of yesterday represent the enormous talent and creativity of the designers of the past, who led the way towards the handbags we see today. They played around with materials, creating bags from substances never before used and experimenting with embellishments by using beads, rhinestones, embroidery and plastics. They explored shape and took into account the needs of the modern woman of their time. Vintage bags can now be found displayed in museums all around the world, an acknowledgement of the important role they have played in our social history. For me, vintage bag collecting is about acquiring those items that represent bygone eras, and owning a bag that has already had a life with someone else. I always say, 'if this bag could talk, what stories could it tell?'. Any vintage fashion piece, no matter if it is a bag, a pair of shoes or a dress, has already brought pleasure to another woman, has already been loved by its original owner and has seen things that we will never get to experience with our own eyes. Collecting vintage pieces is about appreciation of both the item and its past, and buying into the idea that we are keeping something important alive by cherishing its existence.

Whatever you decide is the right path for your own handbag collecting experience, I hope that as we embark on this journey you will be inspired and delighted. You will be introduced to a whole new perspective when it comes to buying handbags, and can revel

It is said that the average woman owns six handbags – I am obviously not an average woman.

in the knowledge not only that your next purchase will bring you joy as you use it, but more importantly that you are personally preserving a piece of fashion history.

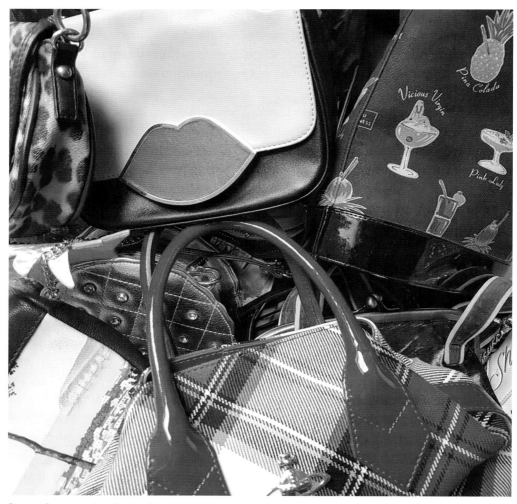

Some of my own handbag collection.

Chapter 2

The History of the Handbag

❧

T he use of handbags dates back thousands of years, to a time when they were made from materials such as animal skins and used as containers for food and flints. Basically, as long as we have needed to carry items, there has been a need to create a vessel to carry them in. However, handbag design has progressed extensively from these humble beginnings, and today bags of every kind are regarded as must-have fashion accessories as well as a simple practicality. Centuries on, we still use handbags to serve the same basic purpose as these ancient civilisations, even if we do tend to fill our much bigger bags with more than just the essentials. We also, like the earliest bag carriers, continue to view our handbags as status symbols, proudly displaying them for all to see. However, we now have a much wider choice in size and design and there are no boundaries as to which bag we choose to show off.

Early pouches

In my previous two books, *Collectable Names and Designs in Women's Fashion* and *Collectable Names and Designs in Women's Shoes*, I made reference to Ötzi, a naturally mummified Tyrolean man from the Copper Age who was discovered on the border between Austria and Italy in 1991. When he was found, he was still wearing remnants of clothing and one shoe was attached to his foot. I mention

A Byzantine relic pouch from the ninth century was found at St Michael's in Switzerland. This bag is lined with red silk and featured embroidered lions on a blue background.

this fascinating discovery again here, as Ötzi was also found with a belt pouch and remnants of a backpack near his body. The pouch, made of chamois hide (an agile goat-antelope found in mountainous areas of Europe), was probably used for carrying some of the smaller of the more than 400 items scattered around the site where he was found. These items include medicinal fungus, flint tools, a needle, an arrowhead and tinder fungus. This groundbreaking discovery has allowed us to learn about ancient clothing and accessories through expert examination of Ötzi and his possessions. It is also proof that as far back as the early Copper Age there was a need for a non-rigid container to transport necessary items around, and it is said that Ötzi's pouch was possibly one of the earliest examples of such an item, making this a significant find.

Handbags started as a men's accessory. Ancient Egyptian hieroglyphics depict men wearing pouches around their waist.

During the Middle Ages there were a variety of bags and pouches used for different purposes and carried by both men and women. In the thirteenth century, small purses called almoners (alms bags) were used to carry coins to give to the poor, while pilgrims and peasants carried bags made of leather and heavy fabric for transporting small goods.

A type of medieval pouch known as a tasque or a hamondey, which was worn hung from the waist, was considered symbolic of status – the more ornate and elaborate

French early fourteenth-century silk, linen and gold leaf embroidered purse. Gifted to the Met Museum by Irwin Untermyer in 1964.

Fourteenth-century French pouch, made of silk and metal thread on canvas and depicting a courting couple.

the pouch, the higher the status of the wearer. These wonderfully decorated bags were generally used to mark betrothal and marriage and were often beautifully embroidered with scenes of love.

Purses with metal hardware came later, with iron clasps and loops that were attached to the belt. This added more security for carrying around valuable items. An early example of this is this velvet bag, with a double pouch and an opening in the front section with the older drawstring closure. At the top is an iron frame decorated with acorns, human heads and lizards, some of which move to release the catches of the opening.

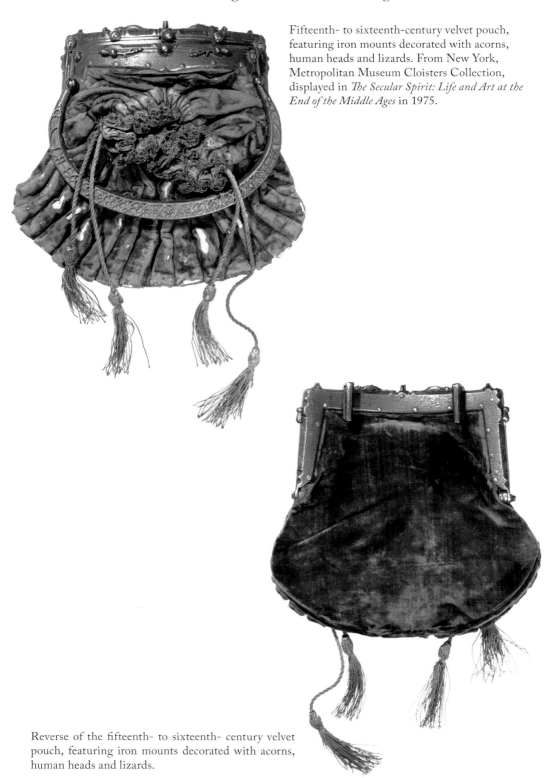

Fifteenth- to sixteenth-century velvet pouch, featuring iron mounts decorated with acorns, human heads and lizards. From New York, Metropolitan Museum Cloisters Collection, displayed in *The Secular Spirit: Life and Art at the End of the Middle Ages* in 1975.

Reverse of the fifteenth- to sixteenth- century velvet pouch, featuring iron mounts decorated with acorns, human heads and lizards.

The sixteenth century and beyond

Swete bags were used frequently during the late sixteenth century and into the seventeenth century by the upper classes. They were so named because they were filled with sweet-smelling materials such as rose petals, spices and oils to overpower

In the late sixteenth and early seventeenth century, the smallest bags expressed the greatest status.

bodily odours and the vile smells in the air. These ornate drawstring bags were handmade and embroidered by highly skilled women who wanted to show off their talents by creating wonderful works of art.

Late sixteenth-century elaborately embroidered swete bag, used to carry scented herbs or essences to cover unpleasant smells. This particular one is made of silk, gold, silver and linen.

Pockets

During the seventeenth century, however, skirts became much wider and fuller, meaning it was no longer practical to hang pouches from the outside of clothing. As a result, pockets were essential and became an integral part of clothing. Worn underneath petticoats, or, in the case of men, beneath the breeches, these pockets were mostly handmade and often given as gifts. Pockets were ideal for carrying small essential items such as jewellery and, for women, vanity items like snuffboxes, mirrors and combs. The pocket was tied around the waist on a string, and there were openings in the side seams of the petticoat so that a lady could easily put her hand through to retrieve that necessary item.

Pockets continued to be worn throughout the eighteenth and nineteenth centuries, even

In the eighteenth and nineteenth centuries, pockets were regularly stolen by thieves who would cut the strings of women's pockets; these thieves became known as 'pickpockets'.

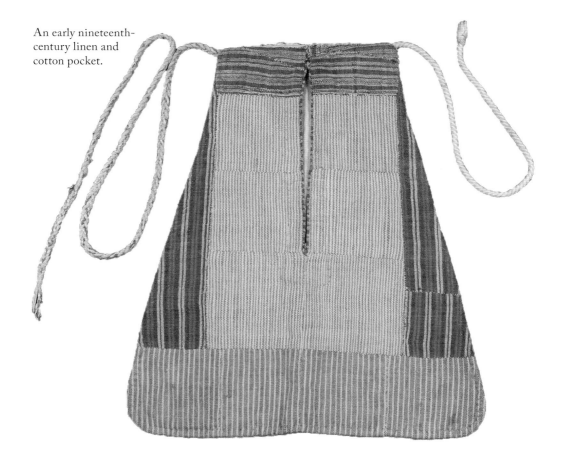

An early nineteenth-century linen and cotton pocket.

though fashion had moved on from large hooped skirts to slimmer silhouettes that hung closer to the body. This was because, even though pockets ruined the line of the dress, they were larger and more practical than the newly introduced reticule bags (also known as indispensables in England),

One of Jack the Ripper's victims, Annie Chapman, was found wearing a pocket containing a small tooth comb and a pocket comb in a paper case.

which were worn carried over the arm. Although highly decorative, these smaller bags were not big enough to carry everything a woman needed.

Pockets in the nineteenth century provided a stark contrast to the pretty, delicately embroidered pockets of previous centuries as they were bigger and lacked decoration. These pockets were practical and were worn either as separate garments tied around the waist or were sewn into the seams of the dress itself.

Chatelaines

The use of chatelaines dates back as far as the Middle Ages. However, the chatelaine was given its official name, which derives from the French word *la chatelaine*, meaning 'wife of a castellan' or 'mistress of a chateau', in the 1800s. It was popularised during the eighteenth century and used into the nineteenth as a functional accessory.

A decorative belt hook worn at the waist with a series of chains suspended from it to hold essential items, the chatelaine was almost always made from metals such as steel, silver or gold. They were typically used to carry watches or other small items to suit the owners' needs, in some cases specific to the owners' duties. For example, a seamstress might have a thimble, a pair of scissors and a sewing kit attached to her chatelaine, while a housekeeper might need

Eighteenth-century gold chatelaine inset with diamonds and featuring intricate enamel work. On the rim of each case there are two eagle heads and the Paris restricted warranty mark.

Collection of cut-steel chatelaine clips.

a variety of essentials including a vesta case, an aide-memoire (notebook) and other useful household items.

The finest chatelaines were very ornate, featuring intricate enamel or repousse work on gold and inset with precious stones. However, most nineteenth-century chatelaines were made from base metal and were extremely functional and versatile.

As the nineteenth century progressed, so, too, did the chatelaine, and variations started to emerge. Instead of multiple items hanging from an elaborate hook, a single chatelaine purse or pocket would be suspended from the chain. This allowed the wearer to carry their few essential items, such as a card case and a handkerchief. Frames were often sold alone,

Close up of one of the beautiful cases from the eighteenth-century gold chatelaine, with enamel work featuring birds, flowers and foliage.

The term 'handbag' was first used in the 1900s in relation to handheld luggage, which was generally carried by men.

allowing the owner to create their own purse from fabrics such as velvet or silk. The frame could be re-used time and time again, so women were able to make new chatelaine purses to match different outfits or if they simply fancied a change.

As with everything, there were also luxurious versions of the chatelaine bag. These were made from precious metals and gems, as in the case of this featured gold mesh purse with a 14ct-gold frame inset with amethyst, diamonds and tsavorites. This particular purse, dating from 1895, is from Marcus & Co., an American luxury jewellery retailer based in New York. It is now part of the Cleveland Museum of Art's collection.

Reticule bags

As I mentioned previously, reticules were the bag of choice in the eighteenth century, especially throughout the Regency period when the fashion was to wear tight-fitting, high-waisted dresses. Originally made from netting and later a variety of fabrics including satin, silk and velvet, the majority of reticule bags were made by the women themselves. A variety of designs and shapes were available – some were knitted, many decorated with tassels, beads and embroidery. This small and lightweight drawstring bag was then carried in the hand or over the arm or wrist on a cord or chain, and as such is seen as the forerunner of the handbag that we know today.

The reticule was another form of bag that remained popular throughout the nineteenth century, but there was now an

Marcus & Co. 14ct-gold mesh chatelaine purse, inset with amethyst, diamonds and tsavorites. Gifted to the Cleveland Museum of Art by Andi and Larry Carlini in memory of Lois F. Cohen.

The word reticule derives from the French term *réticule*, which in turn comes from the Latin *reticulum*, meaning 'net'.

Homemade knitted reticule with beading, circa 1820 to 1840. Part of the Brooklyn Museum Costume Collection at The Metropolitan Museum of Art.

array of other handbag designs on offer. Mesh bags were common for both day and evening usage, as were beaded bags. Small envelope clutches, embroidered and tapestry short-handled bags and, of course, the chatelaine were all part of handbag fashion during the Victorian era. Later, small box-frame handbags made of alligator skin became the essential day bag, a trend that continued into the Edwardian period.

Social and technological advances in the nineteenth century made travel more accessible than ever, creating a whole new demand for a different type of bag. Horse-drawn carriages, boats and trains were the main modes of transport, allowing a greater number of people to traveller longer distances, and as a result larger luggage bags were in high demand. It is from this period in the history of the bag that the term 'handbag' is though to have been coined. Carpet bags, such as the one used by the famous nanny Mary Poppins, were popular among travellers of all classes for use on short journeys. However, a name now synonymous with luxury handbag design recognised consumers' need for quality travel trunks for use on longer journeys. At the tender age of sixteen, Louis Vuitton set out to produce the finest trunks to fill this gap in the market. This venture proved a huge success, and in 1859 increasing demand from discerning travellers allowed him to expand his operation. Thanks in no small part to this early stroke of genius, Louis Vuitton remains one of the most desirable luxury handbag brands to this day.

By the end of the century the handbag had become a fashion fixture that was here to stay. Style, shape, decoration and size would shift with the fashions of decades to come, but the handbag as a concept had made its mark and was now a must-have that no woman could live without. It was now the norm to own a variety of different bags for a range of occasions; women had come to recognise the importance

Edwardian nanny Mary Poppins was never without her famous carpet bag.

Novelty Victorian tartan bag in the shape of a parasol, with a concertina metal hardware opening.

of the style and design of a bag, alongside its functionality.

The twentieth century began much the same as the previous century had ended. Women were still using reticule bags, but the Dorothy bag – a modified form of the reticule – made its first appearance in the early 1900s. The Dorothy was made of softer material but shared the reticule's drawstring opening, always featuring a tassel. Some even had a bevelled mirror to allow the Edwardian lady to apply her makeup while on the move.

Chatelaines, velvet bags, mesh purses, theatre bags and work bags were popular, especially for evening use. These bags were made of materials like dyed suede, decoration was inspired by the art nouveau fashions of the time, and oriental themes were all the rage. Frames were ornately decorated, some hand-carved from ivory or bone, others made from gold, silver or amber. With the arrival of the kissing lock in the early twentieth century, these frames were now able to snap open and closed, providing added security for the ladies' belongings.

In 1901 Louis Vuitton designed a steamer trunk that could be hung on the back of a cabin door. This trunk had a long canvas body and strong leather straps.

An earlier example of a knitted lantern bag with original ribbon trim. Forms part of the Brooklyn Museum Costume Collection at the Metropolitan Museum of Art, gift of the Brooklyn Museum, 2009.

By this point, the handbag had evolved over hundreds of years and was now starting to resemble the bags that we know and love today. However, it was the frivolous, opulent and colourful 1920s that began to take handbag

The Suffragette movement popularised leather shoulder bags.

design to another level. As women grew in confidence, so too did their fashion tastes, and it is in this decadent era that handbag design really came into its own. The vivacious spirit of the roaring twenties worked its way into handbag design, injecting designs with a surge of creativity that continued throughout the twentieth century.

Chapter 3

The Age Of Jazz

'*I adore mesh bags. Even were they not the accepted thing among modish women, I confess to the fear that I would possess one simply to revel secretly in the fascination of its gleaming silken-textured mesh.*'

Catherine Calvert, silent film actress, 1922;
quoted in a Whiting & Davis advertisement

The 1920s is one of my very favourite decades of the twentieth century. Arriving in a burst of colour and vibrancy, the decade in many ways kicked off a brand new era. Long forgotten were the hardships of the war years; instead, a positive future was in the making, especially for the female population now presented with a wealth of new opportunities.

Having been required to tackle traditionally male jobs while their men were away fighting, many women discovered a greater sense of freedom after the First World War. Perhaps most significantly of all, in 1918 women

Actress Lucette Desmoulins posing on a couch in the 1920s.

1920s drum bag, possibly French. Fabric and brass, with an integral powder compact in the lid and diamante decoration.

who owned their own homes were granted the right to vote, and all women over the age of twenty-one gained the vote in 1928. Embracing their newly-won independence and place in society, the female population adjusted their attitudes to life. In few places is this shift clearer than in the clothes and accessories they chose to wear.

Gone were the long skirts of the previous decade. In their place were shorter, more streamlined styles that hit above the knee. This frivolous and exciting new style was epitomised and popularised by film stars like Clara Bow and Josephine Baker, who flaunted the new flapper image of short bobbed hair and even shorter hemlines.

The 1920s handbag was exactly that – a bag held in the hand – but now it was all about fashion rather than function. Although makeup was still not seen as respectable in many circles, powder and rouge were essential tools for the frivolous flapper building her new daring image. As such, these fashionable women generally used their small bags to hold these all-important makeup items, along with house keys and perhaps a few coins.

> ‘If she's a flapper,’ mused the sergeant, wiping Passionate Rouge lipstick off his blameless mouth, ‘then I'm all for ‘em, and I don't care what Mum says.’
>
> Kerry Greenwood, Murder on the Ballarat Train

Handbag styles

Handbags in the Jazz Age were as stylish, colourful and vibrant as the era itself. The beaded bag that had been so popular in previous decades prevailed, mostly used as an evening dance bag. Intricately decorated with bohemian or Venetian beads, these bags were small and often opulent. Produced in vivid colours, the frames were engraved or embossed then embellished with glass, gemstones or enamel. In the early 1920s, most featured metal frames, clasps and handles, but as time moved on handbag bodies and frames became available in early plastics such as Bakelite and celluloid, which allowed for more experimental designs.

Tiffany & Co., along with Van Cleef & Arpels, began to create jewel-encrusted clutches that high society and Hollywood starlets came to covet as an essential accessory.

1920s celluloid compact dance purse with original powder puff, featuring a metal chain and green suede tassel decoration.

The clutch is a style of bag that only became more popular throughout the decade, and has stayed on the fashion scene ever since. Taking the place of the reticule and the drawstring bag, both of which had been carried over from previous decades, the new snap-close clutch was a convenient hand-held size and added a touch of elegance and simplicity to any outfit. This style of bag was also perfect for maintaining that sleek, streamlined look so central to the decade's fashion. A useful and versatile day-to-evening bag, by the end of the 1920s clutches could be found in a variety of animal skins, including snake and crocodile.

> 'Fashion is not something that exists in dresses only. Fashion is in the sky, in the street, fashion has to do with ideas, the way we live, what is happening.'
>
> Coco Chanel

Possibly one of best-known and best-loved bags of the decade, a bag that instantly draws the mind back to the roaring twenties, is the metal mesh bag. The style first appeared in the previous century, when they were made by hand and were, as such, extremely expensive. However, in 1912 A.C. Pratt of Newark, New Jersey invented the mesh-making machine. Thanks to this automation of the mesh-making process, production became quicker and cheaper and these desirable bags were made more accessible. By the 1920s, the style had come into its own and was a must-have accessory for every stylish lady.

Pochettes were another form of clutch, slightly smaller and worn carried under the arm. Designs were available in a vast range of materials, but geometric designs epitomising art deco style were a common theme.

The discovery of King Tutankhamun's tomb by Howard Carter in 1922 directly influence fashions at the time, with Egyptian designs appearing everywhere, including on bags.

Whiting & Davis

The most famous manufacturer of mesh bags has to be Whiting & Davis. Originally known as Wade Davis & Company, it was founded in 1876 by William H Wade, Edward P Davis and Louis Heman in Massachusetts.

Charles Whiting, who had joined the company aged just sixteen, designed the first ever mesh bag in 1892, with all the rings formed and joined by hand. Quickly moving up the ranks, Whiting went on to form a business partnership with Davis and together they raised enough money to purchase Wade Davis & Company, renaming it the Whiting & Davis Company.

In the early 1920s, mesh bags were made of unpainted precious metal rings. Later, to match the vibrancy of the era, more striking designs featuring a mixture of colourful joined rings and metal fringing were produced. Towards the end of the decade, flatter armoured mesh bags painted with bold art deco designs became popular. So, too, did finer Dresden mesh bags, which featured tiny rings that were silkscreened by hand and were available in soft Impressionist shades that turned heads wherever they were carried.

Whiting & Davis were so successful that by the 1930s iconic fashion designers were lining up to collaborate with them.

Bold Whiting & Davis art deco mesh bag with a geometric enamel frame.

Paul Poiret and Elsa Schiaparelli are two designers that are famed for their Whiting & Davis mesh bag designs. Poiret captured Parisian allure in his range of colourful bags, while Schiaparelli introduced modern and exciting shapes to the line. Thanks to the high profile of these designers, stage and screen actresses of the era started to be appear with these Whiting & Davis designs in their hands.

Whiting & Davis 1934 advertisement for *Enamel Tile* mesh bag range.

When the Second World War broke out, production of mesh bags was temporarily halted at Whiting & Davis to allow the company to contribute to the war effort by manufacturing radar equipment. Once the war had ended, usual production was resumed and they continued to make mesh bags and other mesh goods.

'Hand in hand with fashion' was the famous Whiting & Davis slogan during the 1930s.

Whiting & Davis remained popular well into the mid-century. In the 1952 film noir *Macao*, actress Jane Russell wore a dress made entirely of Whiting & Davis mesh in her romantic role opposite Robert Mitchum. This dress is reported to have weighed an incredible twenty-one pounds.

The 1960s ushered in yet another style revolution. The company embraced the mod era with the creation of simple designs featuring cleaner lines. With this adjustment, their mesh bags and clothing fitted in perfectly with the space-age fashion that was popular at this time. The 1970s disco years demanded opulence, extravagance and everything that sparkled and shone from fashion.

Mesh dresses, halter tops and accessories in glittering gold were flying off the rack. With Whiting & Davis successfully promoting their 'soft, sensuous and slithery handbags', they remained at the top of the game when it came

Actress Nicole Kidman carried a vintage Whiting & Davis bag at the 1997 Oscars.

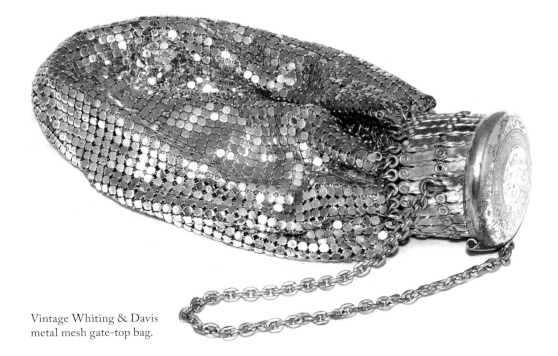

Vintage Whiting & Davis metal mesh gate-top bag.

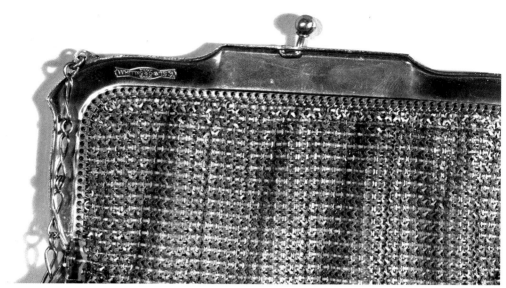

Every Whiting & Davis bag is clearly signed on the clasp.

to producing clothing and accessories, now a popular style statement once more.

According to the timeline on the Whiting & Davis website charting the company's history, the 'excesses of the late '70s slide right into the fashions of the '80s, with mesh accessories and apparel continuing to drape some of the most beautiful bodies of the time'. However, the description of the decade goes on to note an advert describing Frederique Van Der Wal, adorned with glittering Whiting and Davis accessories, as 'Definitely not the girl next door'. In my opinion, this implies that mesh had lost its appeal for the average woman.

Anthony Ferrara, a metal mesh designer, created a dress worth £500,000 out of Whiting and Davis mesh for the iconic Absolut Vodka campaign.

Today, Whiting & Davis are still recognised as a leader in metal mesh handbag design. They are constantly pushing boundaries by introducing new styles, with one eye on the latest trends and the other, as always, on functionality. At their inception, the mesh bags they produced were simple styles made of unpainted ring mesh. Now, Whiting bags are adventurous and exciting, available in an abundance of colours and trims and constantly appearing in the hands or on the arms of A-list celebrities.

Vintage gold mesh purse with expanding gate-top opening.

Mandalian mesh bags

Although we instantly think of Whiting & Davis when it comes to mesh bags, another well-known and respected designer was Turkish immigrant, Sahatiel Mandalia. His Mandalian Manufacturing Company was established in 1898 and began by creating silver-plated handbags and jewellery. They patented their 'lustro pearl finish', a type of guaranteed chip-resistant pearlised enamel, and produced bags that were far more elaborate than their competitors. Taking inspiration from patterns found on Turkish rugs, the designs featured vibrant colours and intricate filigree frames, often lavishly embellished with faux gemstones. Distinctively, the bags mostly were V-shaped, with the bottom of the bag coming to a point trimmed with delicate fringing. I have personally owned a Mandalian bag and have to say that the coloured enamel is just as good as the day it was made – these gorgeous mesh bags are vibrantly colourful and of the highest quality. While Whiting & Davis bags are renowned throughout collecting circles, the Mandalian mesh purses are just as beautiful. They also tend to sell for more money on the secondary market as the company closed in the early 1940s, meaning these bags are becoming harder and harder to source.

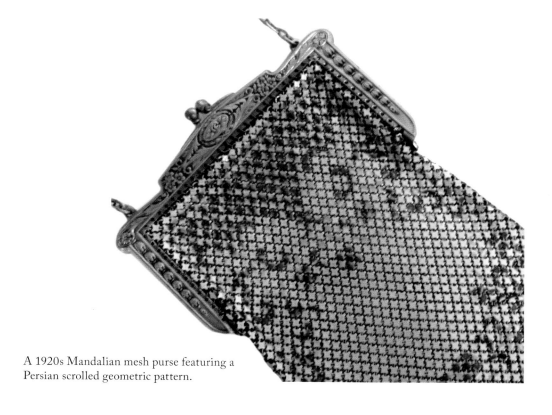

A 1920s Mandalian mesh purse featuring a Persian scrolled geometric pattern.

Collecting tips

The 1920s is an exciting starting point for any would-be bag collector. There is a vast array of designs to choose from, all of which ooze elegance, sophistication and femininity. These bags represent a time in history when everything was loud, bold and beautiful, so what better way to begin your collecting journey than by looking for bags that are evocative of this era? I suggest starting with the delicate and beautiful beaded bags, as these are among the easiest to find and are generally affordable. As with any fashion item, the more opulent the design, the higher the price so start your collection with simpler designs and gradually build up to the more fanciful examples. Always ensure that all the beading is present, that there is no discolouration or fading as can often occur, especially with Bohemian beading, and that there are no tears to the fabric. 1920s clutches are also widely available, and these are just as practical today as they were a hundred years ago. This adds an additional dimension to collecting, as it is so satisfying when you are able to use your vintage bag and show it off with pride. Again, condition is paramount, but in general these bags are affordable and a great place to start building that collection.

As your confidence grows, you can start to branch out into more elaborate bags. Celluloid and Bakelite dance bags and compact bags all epitomise the decadent art deco period, instantly transporting you back to a time of freedom, fun and frivolity. Such bags are in high demand among collectors, who compete against each other to own these interesting and unusual pieces. Prices are on the rise as a result, so make sure you are buying wisely and always check that there are

The 1923 *Bolide* bag was the first Hermès bag to feature a zipper.

1920s black and cream Bakelite flapper bag with diamante decoration.

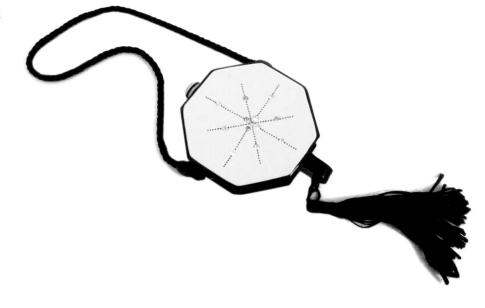

1920s bag featuring a cream daisy pattern and black beaded fringe and decorated with thread and metallic gold tambour stitching. The cord is held in place with mock tortoiseshell rings.

no cracks or splits in the plastic, and that they are in good vintage condition.

When it comes to mesh bags, Whiting & Davis and Mandalian are the labels that command the highest prices. These are the most beautiful and intricate bags that again represent a vibrant era, and generally cost upwards of around £100, with prices constantly on the rise. However, depending on the design, they can be well worth the investment. As always, condition is of the utmost importance with these bags. Although the enamel does hold up well on the body of the bag, there are often components missing, such as sections of the fringing or drops. Links can occasionally come away around the hinges and this will affect the value, so make sure you go over the bags with a fine-tooth comb where possible.

Other 1920s bags to look for include hand-tooled square leather bags, either with or without a strap, tapestry carpet bags and even aluminium enamel bags decorated with geometric designs. In fact, there is such a wealth of different styles and designs to choose from that I couldn't possibly mention them all. Ultimately, I recommend buying what you fall in love with. This is the only way to fuel that passion for collecting, while also guaranteeing that you will never be disappointed as you amass your collection of wonderful 1920s handbags and purses.

Chapter 4

The Glamorous Thirties

'Elegance is not the prerogative of those who have just escaped from adolescence, but of those who have already taken possession of their future'

Coco Chanel

At the end of the 1920s, the world was sent spiralling into the Great Depression after the American stock market crashed. The vibrant times had disappeared, only to be replaced by a dark cloud that hung constantly over this new decade. Frivolous spending was not an option due to high unemployment and the realisation that the threat of a Second World War was just around the corner. In order to escape the harshness of everyday life, people turned their attention to the silver screen. They basked in the glitz and glamour of their Hollywood idols,

My nan (left) with her friend in 1933 wearing casual wide leg trousers and a halter neck top. You can see they are both holding slim envelope clutch bags.

who symbolised a happier way on life. Desperate to inject that same glamour into their own lives, audiences were quick to imitate the style of Hollywood heroes such as Marlene Dietrich, Jean Harlow and Joan Crawford.

The art deco style reigned from the mid-1920s until the outbreak of the Second World War. Its angular and geometric shapes were evident in all art and design forms, from home interiors to architecture and, of course, fashion. The influence of the art deco aesthetic can be found in bags throughout the 1930s. Featuring streamlined shapes and architectural frames, every style of bag paid homage to this exciting new form of modern design.

Most handbag styles popular in the previous decade remained on the fashion scene in the 1930s. Elaborately beaded evening bags and mesh purses remained popular, as did the clutch. Pochettes and slim envelope bags are the bags we associate most strongly with the 1930s, and these were prolific throughout the decade. In this image of my nan walking along the promenade with her friend in 1933 you

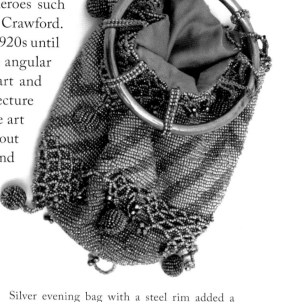

Silver evening bag with a steel rim added a dash of glamour to a night out.

Two delicately beaded 1930s evening clutches.

1930s advertisement for crocodile handbags.

can see that the simple clutch was the ultimate fashion accessory even when out enjoying the day.

This popular handheld bag was geometric or rectangular in shape, designed to be carried against the body. Most were plain and simple in design, with very little or no decoration. The main attraction lay in the materials they were made from, often leather, suede or exotic animal

Arts Décoratifs was a term used after the 1925 International Exhibition of Modern and Industrial Decorative Arts held in Paris. This was shortened to art deco in the 1960s.

Black suede clutch with a hammered silver-tone frame and a contrasting built-in hinged black and white purse.

Interior of the suede clutch, showing the contrasting black and white purse compartment.

skins. Initially these bags featured finger loops, but towards the end of the decade the wrist strap became more common. Although there was a range of colours to choose from, most women opted for plain, conservative colours such as black, brown and white for their day bags.

Women were now having to carry more personal items around with them. To accommodate for this, bags became larger as the decade progressed. Internal compartments for coins, cigarettes, lipstick and other makeup started to feature in designs, allowing the carrier to take all their necessary items with them wherever they went.

Louis Vuitton introduced the *Noé* bag in 1932, following a request from a champagne house for a functional bag that could carry six bottles of champagne safely from A to B. Today, the *Noé* bag is still a classic Vuitton design.

Gucci

One of the most renowned and respected handbag brands of all time is Gucci. Today, the name is synonymous with luxury fashion and the famous *GG* logo instantly identifiable, especially on the fashion house's handbag designs.

Born in 1881, Guccio Gucci wasn't initially drawn to following in his father's footsteps as a leather craftsman. Instead, he travelled to Paris and London. Working as a lift operator at the famous Savoy hotel in London, Gucci was inspired by the high-profile people that he came into contact with. When he returned to his home city of Florence, he began working with his father, making riding equipment to begin with before opening his own leather goods and luggage store in 1921.

As the majority of his clients were horse-owning aristocrats, his initial focus was on the production of equestrian equipment. However, Gucci, like many designers at the time, also turned his attention to creating luxury travel goods for his upper-class clientele. Recognising the importance of horses to the rich and privileged, Gucci came up with a unique touch for his luxury ranges by adding a horse bit symbol to the hardware of his products. This iconic detail is still displayed today on handbags, shoes and other Gucci accessories.

Unique 2014 Gucci *Lady Lock* bamboo handle bag in cobalt blue crocodile with silver hardware. Sold at Christie's online auction in November 2014 for $22,000.

The interior of the Gucci *Lady Lock* bamboo handle bag sold at Christie's online auction in 2014.

Leather was hard to come by during Mussolini's dictatorship, so Gucci looked to alternative materials including cotton, linen, canvas, hemp and burnished cane to make his luxury items. In 1947, the *Bamboo* bag was released; it was to be Gucci's first iconic handbag. Resembling a saddlebag with bamboo handles, this classic bag is still a mainstay of the fashion house.

Bamboo handles are created by a process of heating and moulding. To make one bamboo bag, 140 pieces of bamboo are joined together over a period of two days.

By the 1950s, Gucci was the label of choice among the rich and famous, who proudly brandished their opulent Gucci apparel. After Guccio passed away in 1953, his four sons Vasco, Aldo, Ugo and Rodolfo took the brand to the international level by opening boutiques in London, Paris and New York.

1960s Gucci handbag in *Pigna* pineapple print canvas with bamboo hardware.

The Gucci brand continued to grow throughout the 1960s and 1970s, becoming renowned for their timeless designs. However, facing financial issues and an influx of fakes appearing on the market in the late 1980s and early 1990s, Gucci began to falter. It wasn't until 1994, when American fashion designer Tom Ford was appointed as creative director, that the brand started to recover its status as a leading luxury fashion house.

The double G monogram is instantly identifiable. The two entwined letters represent the initials of the label's founder, Guccio Gucci, and were the brainwave of his son Aldo. Today, this logo is recognised worldwide.

The Gucci green and red striped band is the fashion house's signature look. The equestrian inspiration for this came from the 'web', a special belt used in English horse riding to secure the saddle under the belly of a horse.

'Fashion is born by small facts, trends, or even politics'

Elsa Schiaparelli

Collecting tips

Just like the 1920s, the 1930s is an interesting era to start at with your handbag collection. There is plenty to choose from, and many of the designs from this decade complement current fashion trends. Classic, chic and oozing sophistication, the simple clutch is as usable and on-trend today as it was last century. Examples can be picked up at affordable prices and there is an array of different designs, colours, shapes and sizes to choose

Surrealist fashion designer Elsa Schiaparelli designed some of the most outrageous and forward-thinking handbags of the 1930s. One such bag was shaped like a telephone, and her *Pagan* bag was decorated with suede leaves. Her 1937 *Music* collection featured bags that played tunes when they were opened.

1930s velvet evening bag featuring winged cherub and flower decoration with leather trim, worth £350-£400.

from. The art deco designs are highly desirable with collectors because of their ability to whisk us back to a time when anything seemed possible. Meanwhile, simple mock animal prints have never really gone out of fashion and evoke a point in fashion history when confidence was key and women used their style to celebrate their femininity.

The 1930s were all about glamour, so when you're hunting for bags evocative of the decade go for ones with that little something extra. Keep an eye out for the unusual, such as this featured velvet evening bag decorated with cherubs and flowers. Anything that is slightly out of the ordinary or that features unusual decoration is a magnet for collectors and will hold its value.

Designer examples come at a premium, so although they are wonderful to own, I would suggest steering clear until you have more knowledge about other handbags dating from this period. Visit museums, auction viewings and specialist vintage shops to handle and gain more experience in seeking out those more interesting examples. Read books, look online and speak to specialists in order to deepen your insight into the world of vintage handbags. Learning is a very important part of amassing any collection; the more you educate yourself, the easier it becomes to identify genuine vintage bags as opposed to modern copies and – especially when buying designer bags – outright fakes.

You can further expand your knowledge by visiting museums. The V&A in London, the Bowes Museum in County Durham, the Fashion Museum in Bath and Amsterdam's dedicated handbag museum, the Tassenmuseum, are all must-visits for learning more about antique, vintage and modern bags.

Chapter 5

The Wartime Forties

'Better a good plastic bag than a poor leather'

Vogue Magazine, 1945

With the Second World War having broken out in 1939, the 1940s began in a dark place. Women returned to the usually male roles in the workplace, filling in once again while the men were away fighting. As such, functionality and practicality were paramount when it came to fashion choices, and the handbag was an essential part of this.

The rationing of clothing was introduced in June 1941 to ensure limited resources were distributed fairly. Utility clothing was later rolled out, when it became apparent that the quality and price of rationed clothing needed to be controlled. The government declared it illegal and unpatriotic to embellish clothes for sale, and manufacturers producing utility wear under the CC41 (Controlled Commodity 1941) label were forbidden from using unnecessary buttons, elaborate trimmings or extra stitching on any items, including accessories.

Austerity restrictions on the use of materials, including leather, led to the 'make do and mend' mantra. Wastefulness was not an option, especially where fashion was concerned, so innovative women started creating handbags from alternative materials. Knitted and crocheted handbags became popular, and could be made by anyone using readily available patterns. Bags made from scrap materials also took off. Synthetic fabrics and plastics,

The 1940s saw a surge in knitting, as women were encouraged to contribute to the war effort by knitting for the troops. 'England expects – knit your bit' was a popular advertising slogan.

which gave the look of patent leather, became popular towards the end of the decade, especially in lighter summer colours such as white, yellow and green. This resourcefulness epitomises women's self-sufficiency during the war, and their ability to turn their hands to whatever circumstance demanded of them.

Very rare lady's gas mask handbag from the Second World War, circa 1939. This bag has a normal functioning top with a structured base to house a gas mask.

Another view of
the rare Second
World War gas mask
handbag.

The functional day bag became larger, with long shoulder straps allowing women to go about their daily business without their bag getting in the way. Neutral colours like black and brown were preferred, with outward decoration almost non-existent on day bags. Envelope clutches were still popular, although they contained more compartments for practicality. Ruched and pleated designs became desirable, and shell-shaped bags complemented this new pleated look especially well.

Practicality was of the utmost importance throughout the war years. Following government advice that a gas mask was to be carried at all times, the need arose for a handbag that could accommodate this essential item. Out of this requirement was born a functional but no less stylish type of handbag, featuring a structured base in which a gas mask could be housed. One such gas mask handbag can be seen on the Imperial War Museum website. Here it is explained that masks were generally issued in a cardboard box with string threaded through so it could be

Homemade crochet fan handbags were popular during the 1940s.

carried over the shoulder. Retailers immediately noticed a gap in the market for a more attractive solution, and began manufacturing private purchase containers. These 'could be as elegant and discreetly exclusive as the owner could afford', while also allowing quick access to the mask in case of emergency.

Evening bags were a less sombre affair. Many featured sequins, embroidery and fabric trimming, adding a touch of glamour to the wartime wardrobe. They were smaller than day bags and had shorter straps; small wrist straps were common and the clutch remained a popular evening style. There were a variety of shapes for evening bags; some were round or square resembling vanity cases, others featured ruching and pleating, and many were homemade from materials such as satin, silk and rayon. Evening bags also injected a little brightness into the otherwise dark and austere years, as they were available in a variety of colours and were, as such, more exciting than the plain, utilitarian daytime styles.

The 1940s was a very important decade for fashion, marking a transitional period between the similarly austere 1930s and the more affluent 1950s. 1940s clothing reflected women's renewed freedom outside of the domestic sphere, with women able to wear fashions that represented their strength and versatility. After the end of the war in 1945, there began a slow return to fun and frivolity in fashion.

The practical and utilitarian bags of wartime were replaced with more decorative, innovative and exciting designs. In fact, for me the mid-century onwards is when fashion truly starts to shine and collecting gets really exciting.

Collecting 1940s handbags

There is an abundance of 1940s handbags available to the collector. You only have to glance at online auction sites and vintage shops to see the range on offer. Be aware, though, that 1940s designs came back into style in the 1980s, and some of the bags you find might be from the later decade. Bags that genuinely do date from the 1940s fit right in with twenty-first century style and would complement any modern outfit. However, as when shopping for any vintage fashion, you will likely come across modern replicas, not meant to deceive but simply inspired by the originals. Keep your wits about you and make sure you know exactly what you are buying.

Issue of *Ladies' Home Journal* circa 1948, depicting models posing with their white summer handbags.

Forties-themed vintage festivals take place all over the country – Appleby, Bletchley Park and Woodhall Spa are particular highlights. These events completely immerse you in the era, making them equal parts fun and educational to attend. They offer a great opportunity to talk to other enthusiasts, buy genuine 1940s outfits and accessories and learn more about the wartime years.

Alternatively, there are many dedicated websites where you can buy true vintage 1940s attire. Spend some time browsing the specialist sites and talking to other like-minded collectors – they'll always be happy to advise on what to buy and where.

As with all handbag collecting, the more unusual the design, the more desirable it is. You can pick up basic leather, suede and knitted 1940s bags for as little as a few pounds. Genuine crocodile or snakeskin pieces, however, can go for hundreds of pounds. The summery whites, greens, reds and yellows popular in the late 1940s make a welcome addition to any collection; most of these bags are made of plastics or synthetic materials and can be cheaply and easily acquired. Personal taste is paramount, so shop around and see which designs suit your taste. Buying bags from this era will not make too much of a dent in your pocket but can definitely add a little dramatic flair to your wardrobe.

Chapter 6

The Fabulous Fifties

> ## '*I added two handles to a hard plastic jewellery box and it looked great as a bag, so I took it from there.*'
>
> *Will Hardy*

The post-war years hit fast-forward on fashion. With the gloom of the 1940s lifting and the economy on the road to recovery, designers were free to push boundaries once more. A wave of experimentation with materials, shapes and concepts ensued, freeing handbag design from the restrictions of minimalism and utilitarianism and giving rise to a whole host of innovative and exciting new styles. The golden age of the handbag had arrived.

Handbags were once again must-have fashion accessories. Women no longer owned only one or two practical bags; now, they bought bags to match their entire wardrobe. Whether chosen to complement a favourite outfit or to show off at a particular occasion, handbags were signifiers of a woman's personal style and status once more.

Every material imaginable was used to create these diverse new designs. Straw, wood, plastic, Perspex and metal were all common, and beads, faux jewels, sequins, embroidery

In 1947, Christian Dior launched his *New Look* collection, which was to set the tone for 1950s fashion. Bringing back a feminine silhouette featuring tight fitting bodices and vast skirts with petticoats underneath, Dior's collection set in motion a bolder and brighter future for fashion.

In the fifties, coordinating your outfit and accessories became an important fashion statement. Handbags were chosen to match shoes, belts and gloves.

and even shells were popular embellishments. Styles included the hard-sided box bags that had first appeared in the late 1940s, cylindrical drum bags, wicker basket bags, soft and hard clutches and bucket bags, along with a range of others carried over from the previous decade. With such an eclectic mix of designs and materials on offer, the fashionable women of the fifties were spoiled for choice.

Without a doubt, one of the most famous bags to come out of America in this era was the Lucite bag. Developed in the 1930s by the chemical company DuPont, Lucite is a tough acrylic material made from polymethyl methacrylate, or PMMA. This strong plastic was predominantly used during the Second World War for military purposes, but by the late 1940s it was recognised as an ideal material for jewellery and other fashion accessories. It was in the 1950s that the truly innovative Lucite handbag designs began to appear. The various manufacturers experimented with colour, shape and decoration, with each brand eventually developing their own distinctive trademarks.

Postwar handbag design embraced all things quirky. Designers dreamed up all sorts of fun features, from matching clip-on umbrellas to battery-operated lights that allowed women to enjoy their bags even on the darkest of evenings.

1950s Lucite handbags are often considered 'sculpture to wear'.

1950s Majestic USA Lucite bag with lace detail, clear Lucite lid and handle. Stamped Majestic.

Dorset Rex

The American manufacturer Dorset Rex Fifth Avenue was formed in 1951 following a merger between Dorset Fifth Avenue and Rex Fifth Avenue. The company specialised in high-quality metal and Lucite bags, which are today highly sought after by collectors. Their signature design, featuring a metal

1950s Dorset Rex Fifth Avenue handbag, featuring a grey marl Lucite body and clear Lucite handle. Inside the bag is a full-length mirror stamped Dorset Rex Fifth Avenue.

Dorset Rex Fifth Avenue metal weave bag with toffee Lucite lid and handle. The interior features peach silk lining with a maker's tag.

basket-weave main body, is the epitome of 1950s style. Most Dorset Rex designs were made mainly of metal with Lucite lids and handles, and I have seen some amazing examples with the metal worked into stunningly intricate herringbone and caged patterns. They did, however, also produce some box and barrel bags featuring a Lucite main body with tasteful metal accents in the embellishment and hardware.

Myles Originals

The first manufacturer of Lucite bags in Miami, Myles Originals is another company renowned for their innovative and eye-catching designs. Myles created beautiful Lucite bags, such as the one featured here with a clear carved lid inset with faux jewels, all easily identified by their distinctive three-ball latch clasp. Perhaps most notably, Myles was the first company to use Lamoplex in its designs. Consisting of sheets of plastic with various materials laminated in between, Lamoplex created an unusual, almost iridescent effect. One of the most recognisable types of Lamoplex is the 'crushed crayons' look, which can be found on many Myles bags.

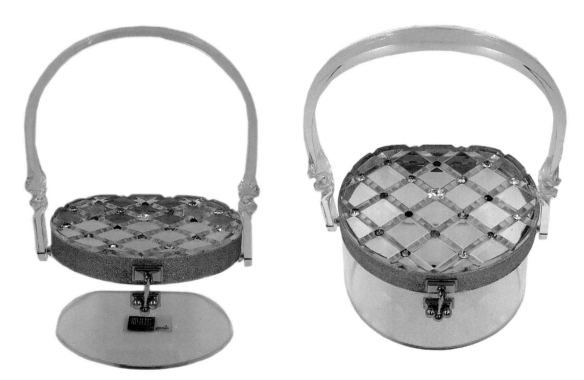

Myles Originals bag featuring a carved clear Lucite lid inset with faux jewels, the distinctive three-ball latch clasp nestled between the brass pegs, and the original paper label.

In 1952, Myles Originals was purchased by the Aberman Manufacturing Company. It is from this point we start to see even more creativity in their designs. Innovations from this time include the swivel-it, a round handle riveted to the top of bag that could rotate for maximum comfort, whether being carried in the hand or on the arm.

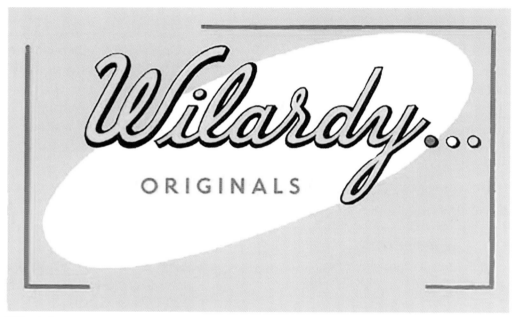

Wilardy logo.

Sheldon A. Aberman constantly pushed design boundaries with his Myles bags, playing with shapes, handles, body decoration and interiors. Some had multiple handles, others removable compacts built into the main body of the bag. All of them were produced to the highest quality; as one of their advertisements stated, Myles bags were 'hand made by fashion-wise, quality craftsmen'.

Wilardy Originals

Of all the Lucite bags that were produced throughout the 1950s and 1960s, my personal favourites are those by Wilardy Originals. Now one of the most desirable brands within collecting circles, Wilardy was the era's largest manufacturers of Lucite bags, operating from 1946 until 1979.

Charles William Hardy and his son William Hammond Hardy originally set up their factory in New York, before moving to New Jersey in 1953. Will was

Llewellyn

There were many other makers of Lucite and other plastic handbags during the 1950s and 1960s, all with their own distinctive designs. Instantly recognisable names include Rialto, Majestic, Tyrolean Inc. and Patricia of Miami, but one of the brands most highly regarded by collectors is Llewellyn.

Operating from Madison Avenue in New York, the Llewellyn line – under the trademark Lewsid Jewel by Llewellyn – produced the most beautiful bags in carved Lucite and shell, a hard plastic made of cellulose acetate. Their bags were inventive and eye-catching, with some of the hard bags looking as if they were soft to touch.

One of my personal favourites is the *Beehive*, which featured a carved lid inset with a trio of metal bees. To this day, this remains one of the most coveted bags by collectors in this field.

Llewellyn *Beehive* Lucite bag featuring a carved lid inset with a trio of brass bees.

Basket bags

It wasn't all about the hard plastic bag during the 1950s, however. Many other styles and designs were also on offer. The straw or wicker basket bag was a popular choice, especially in the summer, and again came in a range of designs. Some were boxy and three-dimensional, showcasing a variety of external decorations. The one featured here, for example, is embellished with real shells, making the ideal bag for a trip to the seaside.

1950s wicker bag with real shells on the front panel.

The plastic coil bag

Another interesting and inventive design to come from this era is the coil bag, also referred to as the telephone cord bag. The style made its first appearance in the 1940s, but this 1955 advertisement tells us that its popularity was in full swing by the 1950s. It was marketed to retailers as 'the handbag that sells itself, offering your customers lightness, washability and a wide variety of colour combinations and shapes.' Imaginative and clearly versatile, this bag design was certainly unlike anything else available at the time.

Rainbow-coloured plastic coil bag, along with promotional material enticing retailers to stock this inventive bag.

Poodle motifs

The poodle was a popular motif in handbag design throughout the fifties. Appearing in many forms and created from a variety of materials, it exemplifies the fun and frivolity in fashion at this time. Some designers took the motif a step further, creating three-dimensional poodle-shaped bags. The rarest of these are by Walborg, a manufacturer that produced a range of hand-beaded poodle purses. These are extremely difficult to find today, and when they do come up for sale they command a premium.

Wicker basket bag featuring a fabric and sequin poodle motif, with a crude Eiffel Tower in the background. This bag could well have been hand-decorated by its owner, as the poodle design is quite crudely made.

This bag, bought by me in a charity shop for £8, features the poodle motif made from small beads and shells.

Chanel

> *'Luxury bags make your life more pleasant, make you dream, give you confidence, and show your neighbours you're doing well.'*
>
> *Karl Lagerfeld*

The 1950s were a time of such innovation and individuality in handbag design, it comes as no surprise that the high-end fashion houses also looked to create their own stand-out signature handbags.

1980s or 1990s Chanel chevron quilted shoulder bag owned by England's first female Prime Minster, Margaret Thatcher. Sold at Christie's in 2015 for £22,500.

The Chanel *2.55* flap handbag is one of the most iconic handbag designs of the decade. This quilted bag, named for the date of its creation, was made of leather with a light but strong gold chain shoulder strap handle, which allowed a woman's hands to remain free while carrying it. The bag also had a hidden zip pocket, ideal for stashing love letters, and

The first designer handbag was sold at Christie's in 1978 during the Coco Chanel sale at King Street. It was purchased by the Smithsonian Institute.

a back pocket designed to hold loose change for tipping, supposedly reminiscent in shape of Mona Lisa's smile. The deep burgundy hue of the interior is said to be inspired by Chanel's childhood uniform at the Aubazine Abbey orphanage. The diamond stitched quilting, meanwhile, was inspired by the equestrian patterns that Chanel had seen around stables.

The *2.55* wasn't Chanel's first handbag creation. In 1929, she had attempted to design a bag with a short chain shoulder strap. Explaining her motivation, she said 'I got fed up with holding my purses in my hand and losing them, so I added a strap and carried them over my shoulder.' Unfortunately, this initial design proved a little cumbersome and even caused some controversy, as women had never before carried a bag in this way.

No stranger to controversy, Gabrielle Chanel constantly pushed boundaries, both in her personal life and her fashion career. Born into a poverty-stricken family in Saumur, France in 1883, she spent most of her childhood in the austere area of Auvergne. Her mother was a sickly woman and her father a philanderer. Life was difficult, and after her mother died of tuberculosis when she was eleven, she was abandoned at an orphanage by her father.

'Women have plenty of roles in which they can serve with distinction: some of us even run countries. But generally, we are better at wielding the handbag than the bayonet.'

Margaret Thatcher

The Chanel black Lucite and crystal rocket ship evening bag was estimated at £6,000 to £8,000 at Christie's in 2019, but sold for £21,250.

Chanel's passion for fashion started at the age of eighteen during her time at the Notre Dame school in Moulins, where she studied the other girls' clothes and fabrics and continued to develop the sewing skills she'd learned at the orphanage. After leaving school she found employment in a lingerie shop and took a second job with a tailor, but she still dreamed of escaping poverty altogether. Intent on finding financial security without having to marry, she knew that rich men would shower her with gifts and introduce to a luxurious way of life. Her dream became reality when Chanel found work as a cabaret singer at a bar. She sang two songs, one of which was called *Qui qu'a vu Coco?*, or *Who has seen Coco?*. This became her signature tune and gave her both a new name and the start of a relationship with Étienne Balsan, a wealthy man whose family had made their fortune in textile manufacturing. It was her relationship with Balsan that set Coco Chanel on her successful fashion journey, and eventually enabled her to open her own fashion houses.

A pioneer of female fashion in what was once a male dominated industry, Gabrielle 'Coco' Chanel was a woman who knew what she wanted and was never, ever afraid to be herself. She revolutionised the concept of *chic*, and her timeless, classic designs ensure that even today the fashion house is synonymous with simple and elegant style.

From the creation of that first *2.55* flap handbag, the Chanel brand was tied to their classic quilted bags in lambskin or caviar leather. Coveted by

Buyer beware – in the 1980s and 1990s the market was flooded with fake copies of the Chanel 2.55 bag, so only buy from reputable sellers and ask for proof of purchase, receipts or any paperwork proving authenticity.

Chanel *Métiers d'Art* Paris-Shanghai black Lucite *Matryoshka* evening bag with gold hardware, sold at Christies New York in 2018 for $32,000. This bag featured in the Paris-Shanghai show in 2010, for which the theme was decadence.

collectors, they are among the top three investment handbags and command huge amounts of money on the secondary market.

Karl Lagerfeld became creative director at Chanel in 1983.

When fashion designer Karl Lagerfeld became creative director at Chanel, the brand started to turn out some far more cutting edge handbag designs. This is especially clear in his twenty-first century work. His inventive designs for the runway were worlds away from the usual chic, quilted bags people had come to expect from Chanel. His novelty offerings included the *Bobbin* clutch from the Chanel Fall/Winter 2016-2017 show and the *Rocket* clutch from the Chanel Fall/Winter 2017-2018 collection. These genius designs were produced in small limited edition quantities and sold out instantly.

In 1984, Chanel began buying small specialist workshops in an attempt to preserve luxury French craftsmanship. These artisans include costume jewellery designers, milliners, feather workers and flower makers, and have become essential in the day-to-day running of the fashion house. Every year, Chanel pays tribute to these ateliers with a special show called the *Métiers d'Art*, meaning 'art professions'. The show, which takes place outside of the usual fashion schedule, showcases the incredible designs and craftsmanship of the house's partners.

Hermès

> *'A Birkin bag is a very good rain hat; just put everything else in a plastic bag'*
>
> Jane Birkin, actress

A French luxury goods manufacturer synonymous with the very highest-end handbags, Hermès produced one of the most iconic bags of the 1950s. While the brand's famous *Birkin* didn't make an appearance until later in the twentieth century, the *Kelly* shot to prominence in the 1950s.

Founded in 1837 by Thierry Hermès, the brand began life manufacturing equestrian harnesses, saddles and wrought iron bridles for the carriage trade. After Thierry's death in 1878, his son Charles-Emile Hermès assumed management of the company, and in 1900 Charles-Emile's son Emile-Maurice introduced the *Haut*

2017 shiny *Vert Emeraude* alligator *Sellier Kelly 25* with gold hardware. Sold at Christie's Hong Kong in 2018 for $101,000.

à Courroies bag. Named for its height and its sturdy handles, the bag was designed to allow riders to carry their saddle with them. A smaller version of this bag was produced in 1922, when Emile-Maurice's wife could not find a handbag to her liking. This version featured a

The *HAC* bag was originally created for cavalry soldiers to store their boots and saddles in.

zip, for which Emile-Maurice secured a patent in France, and is considered the first commercial leather handbag created by Hermès.

When Grace Kelly received the bag for her role in the 1954 Hitchcock film *To Catch a Thief* she instantly fell in love with the design, and is said to have ordered six more to be made in different colours. Two years later, she was photographed holding this large bag as a shield across her stomach to hide her pregnancy, and the

1996 painted white & red *Ardennes* leather *NASA Retourné Kelly 35* with gold hardware by Tom Sachs, 2009. Sold at Christies, London in June 2018 for £40,000.

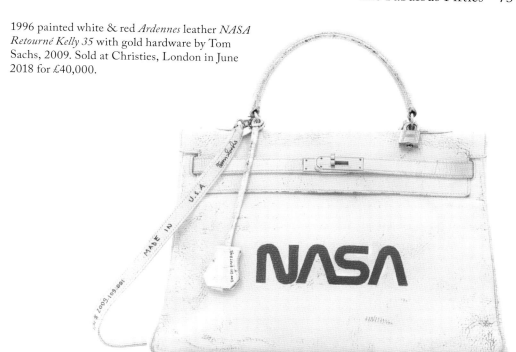

name the *Kelly* was coined. The bag was not officially given this name until 1977, but the 1950s was the decade in which the *Kelly* bag shot to fame.

Since then, this iconic bag has only become more desirable. As with any Hermès creation, though, you might have to wait a while to get your hands on one, as you can't just buy them off the shelf. Each *Kelly* bag is handmade and unique, requiring 2,600 stitches sewn by highly skilled and specialist craftspeople. On average, a single bag takes around twenty-five hours to complete. Orders are only placed twice a year, with the bags generally received six to twelve months later. Stores sell out of them as soon as they hit the shelves – that is, if they were lucky enough to receive any in the first place. This is the case with the *Birkin* as well – such elusive, expensive and luxury bags are near impossible to buy new. My suggestion is to consider buying at auction, as these bags often come under the hammer. Be aware, however, that you could end up paying more than the original retail price, as these are holy grail investment pieces and auction prices are constantly rising.

In 2009, American artist and *bricoleur* Tom Sachs reimagined this featured 1996 Hermès *Kelly* bag. Known for exploring themes of high art and disposable consumer culture in his work, Sachs has said he believes NASA to be the ultimate fashion brand, explaining that he's 'used the NASA logo to help bring authority and power to sculptures.' This NASA-branded bag sold at Christie's in 2018 for £40,000.

The Birkin

The holy grail of handbags, the *Birkin* is just as elusive and exclusive as the *Kelly*. A bag born out of a chance meeting on an aeroplane, today it is the ultimate status bag, adorning the arms of the rich and famous.

Victoria Beckham is rumoured to own more than 100 *Birkin* bags.

The story goes that actress Jane Birkin was sitting next to former Hermès Chief Executive Jean-Louis Dumas on an Air France flight from Paris to London in 1981. The contents of the actress's basket bag spilled out as she was trying to place it in the overhead locker, causing her to complain vocally about the design of her bag. Dumas suggested that she needed a bag with pockets, to which Birkin replied that the day Hermès made a handbag large enough to accommodate all of a woman's belongings was the day she would give up her signature oversized basket bag. This prompted a discussion – and a sketch on an aeroplane sick bag – of what women actually want from a bag. The iconic *Birkin* made its debut in 1984.

The original sketch for the Hermès *Birkin* was made on an airline sick bag.

2014 custom shiny *Gris Tourterelle* and *Bleu Izmir Niloticus* crocodile *Birkin 25* with brushed palladium hardware. Sold for $89,000 at Christie's Hong Kong in 2017.

Rare 2015 matte white *Himalaya Niloticus* crocodile *Birkin 35* with palladium hardware. Sold for a staggering £162,500 hammer price (without premium) at Christie's in 2018.

The Constance

The *Constance*, a hands-free bag, is another Hermès design that ticks all the boxes for brand devotees and collectors. It was designed in 1959 by Catherine Chaille and named after her fifth child, Constance, supposedly because the first *Constance* bag left the factory the day Chaille's daughter was born. Originally made only from box calf leather or *Porosus* crocodile with gold hardware, this design has a leather shoulder strap, a flap top and an H buckle closure.

A success from its inception, the *Constance* was often seen on the shoulder of America's First Lady, Jackie Kennedy, among other well-heeled ladies of status. Over sixty years later this design remains a staple for Hermès. Nowadays, it is available in a variety of sizes, materials and colourways. Limited editions are often released, which only adds to the desirability of the bag. As with

Custom Hermès shiny *Rose Scheherazade* & *Vert Vertigo* alligator *Constance 24* with permabrass hardware. Sold at Christie's Hong Kong, 2018 for $7,500.

all handbags manufactured by this luxury French fashion house, each *Constance* is handmade, meaning no two are exactly the same. Some say that it is harder to track down a *Constance* than a *Kelly* or a *Birkin*.

If you are a serious collector of high-end designer bags, whether vintage or modern, then one of the top three Hermès bags have to be on your wish list. However, for the most devoted enthusiasts (with the best-lined pockets) there is an even more exclusive object of desire. The Christie's website sums up well the allure of the made-to-order Hermès:

'To these collectors, there is no greater privilege than becoming the owner of a bag emblazoned with a horseshoe stamp, denoting that the bag was a special order. To those who can immediately identify an Hermès hue or leather, the special order process remains a significant experience. These one-of-a-kind pieces can drive values sky-high.'

Even those Hermès bags not made to order are still hard to come by; getting your hands on one would be enough to make any fashion-lover's heart happy.

1977 black calfskin Hermès *Sellier Kelly 28* with gold hardware and a 1988 sable ostrich Hermès *Sellier Kelly 32* with gold hardware, sold for $21,000 and $56,000 respectively as part of the private collection of Elizabeth Taylor at Christie's New York in December 2011.

Vintage 1980s Hermès indigo and white leather clutch with shoulder strap belonging to Nancy Reagan, sold for $7,500 at Christie's New York in 2016.

Collecting 1950s handbags

With styles to suit every taste on offer at every price point, the world is your oyster when it comes to 1950s handbags. If fun and creativity are what you're after, this is a great era with which to kick off your handbag collection. Your options are endless – choose from Lucite bags, minimalist clutches or simple day bags for a piece that truly epitomises the era. Those not your thing? Consider knitted bags, drawstring evening bags, wicker or straw basket bags or, of course, high-end designer statement bags. You might want to focus on kitsch designs featuring quirky motifs, like the poodle bags, concentrate on a specific designer or collect a combination of various styles and designs by a whole host of different handbag manufacturers.

It's a good idea to look for quirky, unusual and novelty bags from this decade, as these

When buying Lucite bags, check that there are no cracks, serious surface scratches or damage, as these plastic bags cannot be repaired. Also ensure the bag isn't warped or giving off a strong chemical smell, as this indicates that the plastic is deteriorating. Check that all the hardware is in good condition and still working, and that the lid fits perfectly with no gaps.

will stand the test of time. Kitsch designs and an abundance of jewels and sequins are the essence of this era, and are usually the bags that collectors home in on.

Never be afraid to ask lots of questions before you buy. The more you know, the more confident you will be to purchase. Ask for details of provenance, condition and whether the bag has its original label, as all these points will help you decide if the bag is right for you. Never rush into buying a bag without being 100 per cent sure you know what you are getting.

If you are considering jumping right in at the top end of the market and purchasing a high-end designer bag, such as Chanel or even Hermès, be cautious. Only ever buy from reputable auction houses that have specialists on hand. Christie's is among the best when it comes to selling luxury handbags. They know their market, can point you away from fakes and show you how to invest your money wisely. This goes for any designer handbag from any period, including bang up-to-date contemporary pieces.

As always, it comes down to personal taste and budget, as even some Lucite bags can cost hundreds of pounds if they are by well-known brands or are an unusual design. Try to buy the best you can afford that is representative of the era and you will never go wrong.

1950s Wilardy
scalloped bag.

Chapter 7

The Swinging Sixties

> *'I had to go to Sunday School with white gloves, hat and a handbag, just like a miniature mum in a dress made by her – exactly the same as hers! I mean who wanted to do that? We just wanted to kick against it all.'*
>
> *Marion Foale, fashion designer and co-founder of Foale and Tuffin*

Finally, Britain was back! The economy was booming and a brand new fashion scene had emerged. A time of exciting new trends, subcultures and social scenes, the 1960s was a decade when freedom of choice ruled. This was the era of the Youthquake, a phrase coined by *Vogue* editor Diana Vreeland in 1963 to describe the free-spirited youth movement of postwar baby boomers breaking away from the constraining influence of their elders. A whole generation realised that anything was possible and created a whole new outlook on life, which they expressed through music, fashion and popular culture.

Unprecedented affluence, together with this new disregard for conformity, meant that handbags in the 1960s were a matter of personal choice rather than fashion necessity. The new street style replaced high-end couture and mass-produced fashion flourished in boutiques and stores. These groundbreaking new fashion designs often featured pockets stitched into the dresses, so there was no real need for women to carry a bag. The already-established high-end designers did, however, continued to turn out handbag designs. Although bags were no longer

Cross body bags with long straps became popular in the 1960s.

Mary Quant original daisy logo dolly bag.

a must-have fashion accessory, there were still women who bought them, whether for work or as a style statement.

Good quality, structured handbags with short handles remained popular at the beginning of the sixties, mostly with the older generations who continued to use snap closure bags in crocodile or patent leather. However, handbags were now an individual choice and were no longer an integral part of the total look.

The classic bag was gradually phased out, replaced by brightly coloured pop and illusional op art patterns. Plastic was prevalent, and Paco Rabanne released his chain mail collection covering his entire fashion range, with the bag a reinvention of the previously popular mesh bags. Mary Quant created two dolly bags

Fashion designer Ossie Clark had a small pocket for emergency money sewn into all his dresses, just in case an evening did not turned out as planned.

The Lucite bags that had been popular in the previous decade made the transition, with plastic continuing to be a popular material in handbag design throughout the 1960s.

inspired by op art, one of which featured her famous daisy logo and had a long thin strap that could be worn across the body.

'Fashion is not frivolous. It is a part of being alive today.'

Mary Quant

It was *Time* magazine that first coined the phrase 'optical art' in a 1964. One year later, an exhibition called *The Responsive Eye* was held, and this instantly thrust this new form of art into the mainstream. Op art, as it became known, is a form of abstract art that gives the illusion of movement through a precise use of pattern and colour. Victor Vasarely and Bridget Riley are its best-known exponents.

Psychedelic imagery in vibrant colours on a vinyl vanity bag.

My mum, who was a teenager in the 1960s, recalls that the clothes of the decade were so vibrant that she and her friends were not that bothered about bags. She owned a black one for winter and a lighter one for summer, and that's about it. She does, however, vividly remember the Mary Quant black and white daisy bags that some of the girls owned.

> ## 'Our clothes were so loud and garish that we did not put a lot of emphasis on our handbags.'
>
> My mum, Linda Martin, who was a teenager in the sixties

My mum may not have been a handbag enthusiast back in the sixties (though you'd never guess that now if you saw her wardrobe currently overflowing with bags!), but there were still many fresh and exciting designs to be had. One bag she does remember having is a small, long-strapped bag to hold her lipstick, some change and her door keys, useful for a long night of dancing. Otherwise, she mainly used a larger bag to carry essentials to and from work.

Emilio Pucci

Colour was king in the 1960s, with psychedelic imagery popular on mass-produced and designer bags of all shapes and sizes. Although designer labels were not a must-own during this decade, we cannot ignore the kaleidoscope of colourful abstract graphic prints by Italian fashion designer Emilio Pucci. The 'Prince of Prints' first came to prominence in the fashion world during the 1940s. An expert colourist, Pucci's passion for vibrant colours and bold prints ensured his designs attracted attention. Loved by trend-setting, wealthy women, his signature designs became all the rage in the 1960s and 1970s, as his psychedelic colours fitted right in with the fashions of the day. Not just a passing phase of the psychedelic era, Pucci prints have stood the test of time and are just as desirable today as they were back in the swinging sixties.

Emilio Pucci
print with Pucci's
signature, as
found on all Pucci
prints.

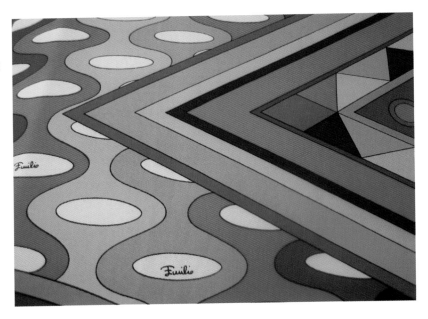

Twenty-first century Pucci bag.

bags are also desirable, and you can find some wonderful Lucite from the decade. Beaded bags are another popular choice and are easily found on the secondary market, as are some fantastic examples of the miniature hatbox bags and shiny patent bags favoured by the mod girls in pastel hues.

There are also the designer options if you prefer to go down this avenue of vintage 1960s handbag collecting. Mary Quant is the designer name synonymous with 1960s fashion. There are only two bags that I know of created by Quant in this era and they very rarely come up for sale on the secondary market, so when they do can sell for upwards of £100 upwards depending on condition. While researching this book I spoke to Becky Robinson, a handbag collector from Kent, who told me a wonderful story about her unbelievable find of these two rare Mary Quant bags:

'I wanted to be Twiggy or Mary Quant at thirteen. Being a bit obsessed with 1960s fashion, I did spend a lot of time altering one pattern into a variety of styles for making 1960s-inspired dresses. I also collected accessories, which included bags, so couldn't believe it when in 1983 I discovered two Mary Quant bags at a boot sale in Deal – I thought I'd died and gone to heaven when I handed over the 10p for both! I did use them when wearing the right dress but was *very conscious of holding onto them tightly, and would always take off the swing tag when using the bag and then reattach it afterwards.'*

These two bags are the epitome of 1960s design and really embody what the decade was all about – exciting, cutting-edge and fresh design.

As always, it comes down to personal taste and budget when it comes to collecting 1960s handbags. Very few of us are lucky enough to stumble across a charity shop or car boot sale find like Becky did, but there are still some wonderful examples of 1960s bags to be found on vintage fashion sites, online auctions and at general auction sales. Some years ago I, too, picked up a fantastic yellow and white plastic daisy bag at a car boot sale, which, although not Mary Quant, definitely fits that same style with the daisy motif. This proves that there are still bargains to be found by vintage-hunters – it just takes a bit of patience and some careful searching.

Although options are more limited than for previous decades, there are still enough designs and styles to satisfy the collector. Look for unusual pieces, such as beaded bags, woven plastics and colourful harlequin bags. These are just as on-

Original Mary Quant handbag label.

Becky's Quant bag, with the swing tag that she would detach when using.

The op art black and white Mary Quant dolly bag that Becky bought at a car boot sale, together with the daisy bag, for 10p.

trend now as they were sixty years ago. As always, ensure the condition is good. Enid Collins bags are prone to losing their jewels and the leather straps often show signs of wear, so always be sure to check these bags over before buying. Beware of scratches on patent bags, make sure all the beads are in place on beaded bags, and check that PVC or plastic bags are not split, brittle or scratched.

Another fun era for handbag collecting, my best advice is to hunt out those sixties bags that are evocative of the decade and reflect the vibrancy and excitement of this momentous time in history.

Becky wearing her Mary Quant daisy bag.

1960s Lucite carryall with integrated compact, lipstick and spare compartment for cigarettes. The mirror pulls forward to reveal another compartment.

Interior of the 1960s evening bag.

Yellow and white plastic daisy handbag from the 1960s that I found at a car boot sale.

Chapter 8

The Seventies and Eighties

'Fashion is very important. It is life-enhancing and, like everything that gives pleasure, it is worth doing well.'

Vivienne Westwood

The 1970s

Handbags in the 1970s were, much like the previous decade, a matter of personal preference unconstrained by strict style rules. It was a time of variety and indecisiveness in fashion. People had a hard time settling on what to wear coming out of the 1960s, with the eclectic mix of styles on offer ranging from glam rock to the hippie movement and Laura Ashely to punk. Miniskirts were still worn, as was the midi-length; A-line skirts became fashionable, and so did wide bell-bottom loons. Everyone was searching for that perfect 1970s fashion statement, but no single definitive trend ever really emerged.

Handbag designs were similarly eclectic. Fringed, tooled leather, basket-weave, plastic, floral, tapestry and beaded bags were all popular, and each material was available in every style, from clutches and cross body bags to bucket and box bags. There was a revival of the 1920s art deco designs, Whiting and Davis mesh metal bags once again were ubiquitous, and novelty bags became a popular choice.

One of the most popular and recognisable novelty bags from the 1970s is the rolled up magazine clutch. Made of plastic and featuring Italian and French magazine covers, it was often seen carried by ladies out dancing at the disco. In recent times, this handbag has made a comeback, with modern reproductions available and celebrities proudly clutching remakes of this iconic design.

Flamboyant dress, makeup, glitter and supersized platform shoes were just some of the diverse fashion statements of the 1970s.

Rolled magazine clutch featuring a plastic frame, vinyl outer, faux black leather strap to secure closure, snap buttons, cotton lining with a pouch pocket and a gold-tone chain handle.

Another rolled magazine clutch bag, with the magazine cover *Primera – Rome – Numero 2* featuring two ladies wrapped in furs.

Dallas Handbags red patent telephone bag with touch-tone keypad and receiver. The original tag is attached: 'Dallas Handbags phone directory. Plug me in, I work'.

Another iconic novelty bag from the 1970s is the plastic telephone bag by Dallas Handbags. A fun predecessor of the mobile phone, you could carry this bag around then plug it into a phone socket and use it as a working telephone to make calls. It came in bright red or black patent, and featured an integrated touch-tone keypad, a receiver handle on the top and a detachable shoulder strap. An absolutely genius design, this is one of my very favourite bags from this decade.

The influence of the hippie movement in seventies bag design can be seen in the popularity of bags hand-crafted from soft materials such as leather and suede. Patchwork was a popular look for suede and leather bags, and fringing and tassels adorned bags swinging from a long thin strap that could be thrown across the body for ease of carrying. Another craft used to decorate these bohemian style handbags was tooled leather – bags of every shape and size could be found with this detailed ornamental work.

Acrylic was also a commonly used material. This durable plastic came in numerous colours, sometimes embellished, and was a fun and funky alternative to the softer fabrics. This image shows a seventies acrylic bag that can be carried with the chain strap over the shoulder or detached to transform it into a cool clutch for the evening.

Brown tooled leather handbag embossed with a floral design.

1970s shoulder bag made of orange acrylic, featuring a gold chain that can be detached to use the bag as a clutch.

Designers

Already-established designers like Gucci, Hermès and Louis Vuitton continued to produce their seasonal collections and remained a mainstay of the handbag industry in the 1970s. However, a new breed of designers also emerged. Some started out with clothing lines before progressing to handbags, while others specialised solely in handbag design.

> *'An iconic, unexpected brand of Britishness. Inspired by the spirit of heritage and the attitude of rebellion. Designed for the everyday lives of contemporary men and women. Made to last.'*
>
> *Mulberry's mission statement*

One of the most iconic and quintessentially British handbag brands to emerge in the 1970s is Mulberry, a label that first appeared on the scene in 1971. Much like Enid Collins, Mulberry's founder Roger Saul began his handbag business from his kitchen table in Somerset. Saul's passion for leather was inherited from his father, who worked for the shoe manufacturer Clarks. His mum invested £500 to help Saul on his way and his sister designed the brand's instantly recognisable tree logo. The name Mulberry was inspired by the trees that Saul would pass every day on his way to school.

Mulberry's immediately identifiable, utterly individualist style was dubbed 'Le Style Anglais' in 1975.

Buckled leather belts were the first accessories that Saul designed, inspired by the classic English country pursuits – hunting, shooting and fishing. These were sold from a stall in London's Portobello Road Market, the humble beginnings of a fashion heavyweight's heritage. Soon, handbags were added to the range, and Mulberry gradually grew from a market stall with just one staff member into the international brand that it is today, now employing over 600 people.

Today, Mulberry is well known for creating It bags. The classic *Bayswater*, named after the leafy area in West London, is one of Mulberry's most iconic bags and has remained popular with women since its creation by designer

Mulberry bestseller the *Alexa* bag was named after TV presenter and model Alexa Chung.

Nicholas Knightly in 2002. Considered the first ever Brit It bag, the *Bayswater* remains a staple in the Mulberry collection. It has been described as a hybrid of an English doctor's bag and a structured Hermès, and is available in a range of sizes and colours. Recently, the classic design has been revisited by the brand's current creative director, Johnny Coca. Coca's revisions include the addition of branding under the flap, as some people prefer to wear the *Bayswater* with the flap tucked in.

The *Alexa* debuted in 2009. Named after model and TV presenter Alexa Chung, it was available in a vast array of leathers, sizes, colours and patterns, from animal print to

The earlier Mulberry designs were inspired by English country pursuits – fishing, hunting and shooting.

Mulberry *Small Darley Satchel* in a vintage-inspired shape featuring seasonal tartan print and stud detailing.

Mulberry postman's lock, as featured on the *Darley*.

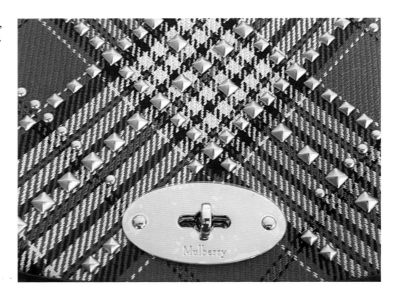

tweed. Its reign finally came to an end in 2017 when it was discontinued, making it a sought-after style with collectors today.

Another classic Mulberry bag, the *Iris*, was 'designed to shine as an everyday favourite.' You can personalise your *Iris* bag by buying additional interchangeable braided top handles, making it a fun and versatile choice. The *Amberley*, my personal favourite of all the Mulberry bags, brings us back around to the 1970s. Launched at London Fashion Week in 2017 and named after a twelfth-century castle in Sussex, it was inspired by two of the brands original 1970s designs, the *Trout* bag and the *Poacher* bag.

Rounding out the classic designs of Mulberry's luxury range are the *Lily* and the *Darley*. Both feature the brand's signature postman's lock and come in an extensive range of styles, colours and sizes.

Mulberry has secured its place as one of the most important names of the twentieth and twenty-first centuries in British handbag design. Quality craftsmanship combined with fascinating heritage has ensured that this brand has gone from strength to strength since its inception in 1971, and for this reason alone Mulberry should definitely be on your handbag hit list if you can afford to invest in one or two.

The 1980s

An era of big hair and even bigger shoulder pads, the 1980s were all about power statements. In stark contrast to the seventies, this decade knew exactly what the name of the game was – status, wealth and success. As a teenager in the 1980s, I

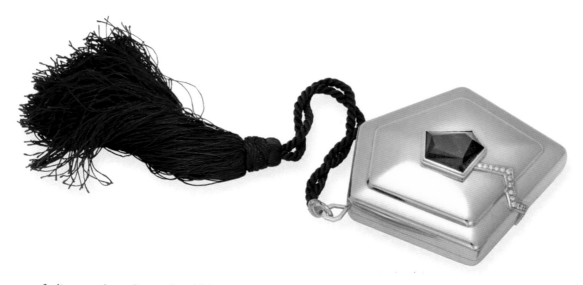

Italian amethyst, diamond, gold & platinum evening bag, designed by Paloma Picasso for Tiffany & Co. 1985. This bag reached a world record auction price for any Tiffany & Co. evening bag, selling for a staggering $20,000 in New York in 2011.

have vivid memories of this large and in charge time in history. True to the towering aspirations of the era, my mum's wardrobe was full of sky-high stilettos and bags to match. Calling myself a 'casual', my own tastes initially leaned towards knee-length skirts paired with canvas slouch boots, before moving on to the classic voluminous hair and oversized shoulder pads. This was a time when every fashion choice made a bold statement about the wearer, and every out-there look needed a statement handbag to match.

The economy was booming and success was the buzzword of the day. This was especially true among yuppies (short for young upwardly mobile professionals), a new breed of urban middle-class young people keen to showcase their wealth through the luxury items they owned and the designer labels they wore.

You needed to stand out, make a statement and be noticed in the eighties.

Designers were thrust back into the limelight, with Christian Lacroix, Karl Lagerfeld, Moschino, Versace and Yves Saint Laurent central to the 1980s fashion scene. Couture was once more in vogue, the bigger

Pop idol Madonna was renowned for her crazy eighties fashion, best described as post-punk meets New Romantic. Neon lace tops layered over a bra and lace leggings paired with studded ankle boots – her style was truly unique and is now a look inextricably tied to this era.

the price tag, the better – flaunting your wealth was not only encouraged, it was expected.

Designer handbags were a must for every upwardly mobile woman. Unlike the previous decade, they were free from embellishments and generally very plain, unless they were covered in the designer's logo or dripping with logo-emblazoned hardware. Basically, it was all about the name and the size – nothing in fashion was subtle in the eighties.

Chanel, Dior, Gucci, Hermès and Louis Vuitton were the designer heavyweights of the decade, but brands such as Dooney and Bourke, Coach and Vera Bradley rose in popularity as a slightly more affordable alternative for the a wider consumer base.

Colour was crucial; red was the popular pick early on, overtaken by metallic golds and bronzes towards the end of the decade. However, the colours that have come to define the era are the brightest and boldest. Electric blue and fuchsia pink, neon orange, fluorescent greens and yellows – these are the colours that we now think of when revisiting this decade.

Vivienne Westwood

The decades-spanning career of one of my all-time favourite designers, Vivienne Westwood, began in the 1970s with her first shop selling second-hand clothes.

In 1965 Westwood met Malcolm McLaren, the man who would launch her career. He was the founder and manager of the punk band the *Sex Pistols*, and together he and Westwood opened their first clothes shop, Let it Rock, in 1971. With hippie fashion on the way out, the pair were drawn towards the harder-edged teddy boy looks and rocker gear.

They renamed the shop Too Fast to Live, Too Young to Die, complete with a skull and crossbones logo, and Westwood began to work on her own designs, selling them alongside the second-hand garments. She ripped and cut holes in plain t-shirts, and added studs, chains, nipple revealing zips and even chicken bones.

> *'Fashion was a baby I picked up and never put down.'*
>
> Vivienne Westwood

They renamed the shop once again in 1974, this time to Sex, and sold aggressive, explicit and anarchic clothing. It was after a further name change, to Seditionaires, in

1979 that McLaren and Westwood made their transition from fetish garments into mainstream fashion. A final name change to World's End saw Westwood (with some input from McLaren) start to design her own fashion lines, mostly inspired by historical influences. The *Pirates* collection, one of her most famous, launched in 1981 and was influenced by seventeenth-century dress.

McLaren and Westwood parted ways in 1982, and in 1983 she launched her first solo collection, *Witches*, inspired by New York graffiti artist Keith Haring.

Westwood's famous *Yasmine* bag first graced the catwalk in the Autumn/Winter Gold Label 1987/88 runway show *Time Machine*, and later appeared in shows such as *Café Society* Spring/Summer 1994 and *Anglomania* Autumn/Winter 1993/94.

Vivienne Westwood red tartan *Yasmine* bag.

Close-up of Westwood's orb logo.

Vivienne Westwood *I Love Crap* clutch bag, 2013.

This iconic bag was named after the French designer Yasmine Eslami. Eslami worked for Westwood in the 1980s and carried the first prototype of the bag to hold her essentials – cigarettes, lighter and lipstick.

Vivienne Westwood's logo is the orb.

Today, the *Yasmine* is still a staple of the Westwood collection and has been produced in every imaginable colour and design over the years. Recently, the *Mini Yasmine* was released, a smaller and completely vegan version of this classic design.

I always suggest Westwood if you are looking for something slightly different. Her handbag designs are classic but also sometimes a little outrageous and most definitely quirky. Take the 2013 *I Love Crap* clutch bag, for example, which was handmade from recycled materials in Nairobi. This bag formed part of a special collection of accessories by Westwood in support of the Ethical Fashion Initiative, a scheme providing paid work for thousands of women living in extreme poverty. This bag is one of my absolute favourites, as not only was it created in support of an amazing cause, it has that signature Westwood cutting-edge flair that makes it stand out from your conventional clutch bag.

Hunt out vintage Westwood bags but don't dismiss her modern designs. They are all worth investing in as iconic fashion collectables.

Collecting 1970s handbags

Just as with the previous decades, there is much choice when it comes to collecting bags from the 1970s and the 1980s. There were plenty of high-end designer offerings throughout the era, but cheaper options are also available to the avid collector.

I like the hand-crafted patchwork and fringe bags of the 1970s, as they epitomise the free-spirited hippy era, but I'm also partial to the disco goer's rolled magazine

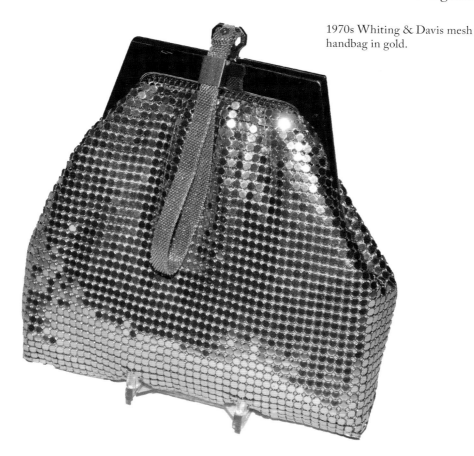

1970s Whiting & Davis mesh handbag in gold.

clutch. I always favour novelty designs, as they speak to me more than classic design. Although I of course appreciate the classics, I do like my bags to stand out. There is nothing more exciting than a vintage bag that takes centre stage when it's used, as other people admire its unusual design.

With rolled magazine clutch bags it is important to ensure they are original 1970s pieces and not more modern replicas. The price difference should indicate the age – a genuine 1970s magazine clutch can cost from £100 to £200, while a reproduction will be around £20 to £50.

Seek out other interesting 1970s bags from reputable online vintage shops and online auctions. The rarer examples, such as the Dallas Handbags telephone bag, do occasionally come up at general auction. You can use the site www.the-saleroom.com to hunt out bags due to come up for auction all over the country.

Whiting & Davis mesh bags were everywhere, often teamed with the lamé outfits favoured by the disco goers. These bags will always be popular with collectors, and if you are unable to afford the earlier examples from the 1920s then the versions from the late 1970s and early 1980s are the perfect alternative.

When it comes to buying any designer bag, you need to check authenticity. There are many 1980s fakes on the market, especially for Mulberry and Chanel. Only buy when you have proof of purchase, provenance and are certain you are dealing with a reputable seller who can guarantee the bag is genuine. Buying new pieces from the designer's website is always an option, and in my opinion is the best way to go if you're looking to invest your money.

An eclectic decade with a mishmash of styles and trends, the 1970s is a great area for collectors, as you can research the various trends and decide which best suits your personal taste. It is also a trip down memory lane, as you relive the glam rock, punk, hippy and disco days of a decade that was full of feminism and frivolity.

When it comes to the 1980s, it can be slightly more difficult to find show-stopping pieces, as most bags from this era are very plain. On the more positive side, they are cheap to buy. Look for vibrant colours, metallics or something that instantly screams eighties. There's also the option of buying designer bags from the era, the most popular and affordable of which are the Gucci logo bags. These were very desirable in the 1980s and come up for sale often, with a price tag that isn't too steep.

Other designers to look out for include Moschino, Jean Paul Gaultier, John Galliano and Karl Lagerfeld.

Collectable Lulu Guinness *Sophie Fan* clutch embellished with pearls.

Collecting Lulu Guinness bags

Lulu Guinness handbags are hugely popular on the collectors' market, especially the limited edition examples such as the *Sophie Fan*, the 1998 *Spider's Web*, the 2003 Schiaparelli-inspired *Lobster Dress*, the 2002 *Circus Tent* and the stunning 2009 automated *Birdcage* bag with singing bird, released to celebrate the brand's twentieth anniversary. If you manage to source any of these on the secondary market through online auction sites, snap them up – they make a fantastic investment.

You might be lucky, as I was when I found a Lulu Guinness bag at a car boot sale, spotting its cocktail print from across a crowded field. I'm sure you can imagine my celebrations over a cocktail or two that evening, having paid just £1 for such a stunning handbag. This proves that there are still bargains to be had out there and that not everyone understands the importance of Lulu Guinness handbags, so keep your eyes peeled in charity shops and at your local car boot sales.

Another way to acquire these must-own bags is by checking out the Lulu Guinness sale, held twice a year in summer and winter. I have bagged (pardon the pun) some fantastic examples of her work at discounted prices this way. I have also taken the plunge and bought her bags at full price. Just now, I have pressed the 'pay now' button and purchased the limited edition *Miranda* wheat straw basket bag from the 2020 *Ladies of Lulu* collection. Topped with fruit-basket detailing and a heart-shaped mouth, this gorgeous bag wasn't in the sale but I just had to have it. As I have said, it is a sound investment for the future – well, that's what I'm telling myself, anyway!

Lulu Guinness silver snakeskin effect *Lips* clutch bag. The *Lips* clutch is now a classic Lulu Guinness design.

The Lulu Guinness *Friendship, Love and Truth* bag.

The Lulu Guinness 20th anniversary automated singing *Birdcage* bag, 2009, was the world's first singing handbag. It also had a secret drawer made to fit a lipstick

2002 Lulu Guinness *Circus Tent* bag.

The Dior *Saddle bag* is one that I remember. Although a relatively short-lived style, this saddle silhouette was made popular (as so many bags, including the Fendi *Baguette*, were) by the character Carrie Bradshaw in the hit TV series *Sex and the City*.

Fendi released their *Baguette* bag, so named because it was designed to be worn as if carrying a loaf of French bread under your arm. This small yet stylish bag was comfortable to wear and became another celeb favourite, earning it It bag status. In fact, demand for this pochette bag outstripped supply, creating waiting lists of women desperately wanting to get their hands on one.

Limited edition Louis Vuitton monogram canvas 1998 France World Cup football with nomade leather carrier (not pictured).

Other established fashion houses continued to release their seasonal collections throughout the nineties. One of the most interesting offerings of the decade was Louis Vuitton's limited edition bag commemorating the 1998 France World Cup, a monogrammed canvas football with a nomade leather carrier. An example of this rare and special piece came up for auction at Christie's Hong Kong in May 2017, selling for a staggering $13,000.

Chapter 10

The Millennium, the Noughties and Beyond

A new century – and a new millennium – had dawned. Handbag design had come on leaps and bounds over the previous decades and there was no stopping this progression once the millennium had arrived. Bags were by now cemented as so much more than functional apparel for carrying necessities – the It bag defined social status, novelty bags remained popular, and today anything goes in handbag design, from small pochettes and large totes to cross bodies and backpacks. There is quite literally a bag for every taste and every budget.

With endless styles and hundreds of designers to choose from, I will simply highlight some of my personal favourites, the bags that I feel are not only collectable now but have the potential to become especially desirable in the future. These bags showcase the immense talent of their designers, who compete to produce the most innovative displays of creativity in their designs from high-end to high street.

Irregular Choice

'Originality in design'

Irregular Choice's motto

Well known for their wacky, off-the-wall shoe designs, Dan Sullivan's Irregular Choice also offer some of the most fantastic and original handbags on the market. Many are licensed branded products, such as their *Disney* collection. These ranges in particular are instant hits with style-savvy shoppers and fashion collectors alike.

The brand's fantastically bizarre yet mesmerising handbag designs were first introduced in 2004. Ever since, they have captured the hearts of those handbag obsessives eager to own something completely unique. Working with quirky shapes, unusual fabrics and plenty of embellishment, Irregular Choice offer some of the most showstopping designs on the high street.

Amore, *Zevra* and *Up Up and Away* are just a very few of the amazing handbags you will discover when delving into the wondrous world of Danny Sullivan's

Irregular Choice *Cross My Heart* robot bag.

Irregular Choice collections. There is a bag to please even the pickiest collector among his stylish yet limitlessly inventive designs. An impressive array of styles and materials and an extravagance of embellishments ensures that

Dan Sullivan's parents created crazy footwear throughout the 1970s, 1980s and 1990s.

every Irregular Choice bag is a unique visual treat, making the brand a firm favourite of those fashion-forward enough to appreciate a healthy dose of individualism.

Up Up and Away, one of the two Irregular Choice bags released in 2019 to celebrate the brand's 20th anniversary. The hot air balloon design, featuring appliqué, a miniature basket and some of the brand's iconic prints, was described as having fans 'floating in the clouds with Irregular Choice nostalgia'.

Sullivan was born into the design world, reminiscing about his parents talking fashion around the dinner table when he was a child. He spent much of his youth being taken to trade fairs, shoe factories and retail stores, where he was stuck in a corner waiting patiently while his parents attended meetings.

It was on one of these business trips visiting Italian shoe factories that Sullivan sketched his first shoe design. His parents loved it so much they placed the design into production, the first of several of his designs they would manufacture. However, he only began to learn the art of shoemaking after he had left school. His parents shirked conformity in their work and developed their own distinctive styles, a quality inherited by Sullivan and evident in all of his shoe and handbag designs.

Irregular Choice 20th anniversary *Bon Anniversaire* bag with printed scarf.

Taking his inspiration from anything and everything, Sullivan feels that design – like life – is all about perception. A group of people might all look at the same item but each see it in a completely different way. Sullivan likes to look at everything through a cute, fun and, well, irregular lens, which he then transfers to his bag designs. To him, this is the essence of what Irregular Choice is all about.

Sullivan founded Irregular Choice in 1999, aged just 28, and he hasn't looked back since. Over twenty years later, the brand continues to go from strength to strength. With the introduction of the handbag ranges and other accessories, the brand has become a fashion force to be reckoned with.

Irregular Choice released two handbags to celebrate their twentieth anniversary in 2019. The *Up Up and Away* bag was shaped like a hot air balloon, and the *Bon Anniversaire* bag featured a birthday cake in the middle with twenty candles and the special twentieth anniversary print, plus a detachable printed scarf. These two designs, like all his others, were an instant success and sold out quickly. Now, they are highly sought after by those who were unable to snag one when they were released.

Collecting Irregular Choice

Irregular Choice is already very high on the collector's radar, with many people desperate to get their hands on latest collections or eagerly seeking discontinued designs. Some brand devotees buy as many Irregular Choice pieces as their budget will allow, while others prefer to cherry pick their own personal favourite styles.

The other compelling reason for collecting this brand is its affordability. The option to buy kooky and elaborate designs produced to the highest standard for considerably less than your average designer handbag makes Danny Sullivan's work a magnet for collectors.

Panthera is a sequin-tastic Irregular Choice backpack featuring a leopard print effect.

Reverse view of the Irregular Choice *Panthera* backpack.

As always, look for the brand's limited edition handbags, along with the licensed bags that are only around for a short length of time and are discontinued quickly.

When you buy an Irregular Choice handbag you are not only acquiring a completely unusual and attention-grabbing new piece for your wardrobe. You are also investing wisely, as Irregular Choice handbags are highly sought after on the collectors' market and, as an important part of British fashion heritage, have the potential to increase in value over the years.

Radley

I have always been a fan of Radley handbags, especially the designs that feature their signature Scottie dog motif with appliqué work. British made, the brand started out in Camden Market in the heart of London when founder Lowell Harder decided to make a career change from architect to handbag designer.

Radley *Market Day* bag showing Radley running his market stall selling fruits and flowers. Released in 2015, this *Signature* bag features a pastel colourway and appliqué in the foreground.

Initially, Harder imported bags that she had designed and had manufactured in India, selling them on her stall in the market under the name Hidesign in the 1980s. It wasn't long before the bags were a huge success and she was approached by retailer John Lewis, who wanted to stock her products. This was a fantastic opportunity, but it did mean that Harder would need some help financing and completing the orders. She approached Tula, a well-known handbag manufacturer, and they agreed to help, allowing Harder to expand her horizons and begin experimenting with fun, colourful designs. Unfortunately, retailers at the time saw toned-down handbags as more marketable. Harder responded to this commercial requirement and her brand became an immediate success.

The brand name Radley was created in 1998. Back then, the brand's bags were quite different to the bags that we associate with Radley today. There were no vibrant designs, instead focusing on neutral, conservative colours for a simple yet

Radley *Make A Wish* bag, released in 2014, showing Radley and his friends on a rooftop gazing into the night.

stylish look. However, colour did gradually start to creep in, whether in the lining, under the straps or in other tiny details in the design.

Radley says their approach is simple – to create the perfect combination of style on the outside and functionality on the inside. They achieve this by blending creative design with quality materials, talented craftsmanship and plenty of personality.

Today there is an extensive range of Radley bags to suit all tastes. Yes, you can still buy the chic and neutral monochrome designs, but there are also the picture or *Signature* bags. These are the bags that I love best, and are the ones that have attracted a dedicated following among collectors.

The picture bags first made an appearance in 2002 and have since become known as the *Signature* bags. The *Beach Hut* and *Penguin* designs were the very first, followed by *Gnomes*, *Beach Huts* and *Armchair* in 2003. Radley continue to release their picture bags twice a year, once in the spring/summer season and once in the autumn/winter season, along with the odd limited edition creation.

The Scottie dog signature was created as a representation of the brand's British roots and sense of playfulness.

Walk in the Woods, released in 2007, was a very limited edition of just 250 grab bags and 250 tote bags and as such is very desirable on the collectors' market. The fourteenth bag to be released, it features the Scottie dog Radley walking in the woods with a little girl. She is carrying a stick that Radley is waiting for her to throw. This particular bag could only be purchased in the London stores, making it a rare piece that commands as much as £450 on the secondary market.

One of my personal favourites has to be *Under the Mistletoe*, released in 2015 and available as a grab bag, clutch or large zip matinee purse. In this design, Radley is sitting with his companion in front of a Christmas tree, holding mistletoe in his mouth. It was created by illustrator Rachael Saunders and is a wonderfully festive bag.

Make A Wish is another design that I particularly love. Released in 2014, it depicts Radley and his friends sitting on a rooftop and gazing into the night sky. Although not a limited edition, meaning thousands of the bags were made, it is still a lovely design that again shows how Radley have mastered the art of creating wonderful appliqué scenes on the body of a bag.

In general, Radley bags released in large edition sizes are not especially collectable. However, some of the early *Signature* bags can command a premium on the secondary market, as can the special limited edition designs.

Yoshi

When it comes to unique design and masterful craftsmanship in picture bags, another brand that instantly springs to mind is Yoshi. They, too, have produced some stunning designs over the years. Much like Radley, they have an essence of fun, which they express through a variety of different scenes and images on their leather goods.

A small family-run business, Yoshi was born from a fusion of the culture of Osaka (a city in the Kansai region of Japan's main island, Honshu) and a British penchant for quality and design. There are over fifty years of experience in product design, manufacturing, and the handcrafting of leather within the brand. It is no surprise, then, that when they launched their first collection in the winter of 2006 it was an outstanding success.

An homage to the literary classics, the Yoshi *Bookworm* shoulder bag features a collection of leather appliqué books.

Yoshi *Be Kind Rewind* shoulder bag, offering a step back in time to when we could record our own movies. The VHS video cassettes are carefully handstitched onto the front.

The brand states that in buying a Yoshi product, you do not just become the owner of a beautiful leather bag or purse, you become part of both the history and the future of the Yoshi brand. And what a brand to be a part of – a family business that produces stunning, well-crafted handbags that will last a lifetime.

Yoshi declares that all of their leather bags and purses are designed and handmade with love, attention to detail and a little bit of hard work.

Of all of Yoshi's creations, a few bags in particular stand out to me. The *Bookworm* range is completely original, featuring appliqué books on the front, from classic novels to modern literature. *Be Kind Rewind* is another of my favourites, as it whisks me back to a time when playing a movie on the VHS recorder was a family affair. This bag instantly transports you back to happy and nostalgic memories that you can carry around with you forever.

Another hit novelty range is *Biscuits*, which pays homage to some of Britain's favourite biscuits. Jammie dodgers, custard creams and bourbons are recreated as purses, pouches and cross body bags.

As with other picture handbag manufacturers, these bags are popular with those looking for something a little more unusual, and with all of Yoshi's collections you are certainly getting something different. Oozing quality yet still firmly on the fun side, these bags will make you smile every time you carry one.

The Yoshi *Bourbon* cross body pays homage to one of Britain's favourite biscuits. In chocolate brown leather, it is a fun and quirky bag.

Kate Spade *Rose Camera Bag*, S/S 2020 in *Fiji Green*. The bag resembles a vintage camera and even has a hidden pocked in the lens.

55. Her husband revealed that she had been suffering with depression for some years but that there had been no indication that she was going to take her own life. Kate's untimely death caused devastation in both the fashion industry and the public, with hundreds of people relaying their 'Kate Spade moment' of buying their first handbag. This exceptional designer has left behind an impressive legacy, as her name will forever remain synonymous with exquisite accessory design.

Anya Hindmarch

Essex-born Anya Hindmarch is another leading British handbag designer who, aged just 19, opened her first shop from a small unit on London's Walton Street. It all began on a trip

Anya Hindmarch bags all feature the trademark bow logo.

to Italy, where she discovered that small drawstring bags were all the rage and believed the trend could catch on with women back in the UK. Coming from an entrepreneurial family, Hindmarch borrowed some money and had the bags manufactured in Italy. She sent one off to the fashion magazine *Harper's and Queen*, and when they featured it she received 500 orders.

Inspired by Prime Minister Margaret Thatcher, Hindmarch saw herself as an Iron Lady in her own field. After the success of the drawstring bag she began to design her own handbags, and today she has stores all over the world, including her two flagship stores in London.

Anya Hindmarch green *Walkers* crisp packet evening bag featuring sequins and beadwork.

I queued from 5am to get my Anya Hindmarch *I'm Not A Plastic Bag* bag.

Hindmarch prides herself on her brand's beautiful craftsmanship and attention to detail and has won many awards for all her achievements. Her handbag ranges still include the drawstring bag that launched her career, along with her bespoke handbag ranges, classic styles and novelty sequin-covered evening bags in the form of Walkers crisps and Cadbury chocolate.

Anya Hindmarch was named Accessories Designer of the Year at the British Fashion Awards in 2001 and Designer Brand of the Year at the 2007 awards.

One of the best-known of Hindmarch's bags is the *Ebury*. A design of simple structure featuring signature interior pockets, a maxi zip fastening with a tassel and a detachable strap, this bag has become a timeless classic. Hindmarch has even launched the *Bespoke Ebury*, a service allowing customers to choose their own colours and sizes. This bespoke bag also comes with a customisable message embossed inside the bag, fully personalising it to the owner. The bespoke service also includes fun vintage touches such as a lucky penny in a wallet.

In 2007 Hindmarch collaborated with social change movement We Are What We Do to produce a tote bag with the slogan 'I'm Not A Plastic Bag', as part of a campaign to end the use of plastic bags. These bags were available from Sainsbury's for £5 each but numbers were very limited instore. I know this because I was one of the people that queued outside my local Sainsbury's store from 5am on the day of the release to secure one for myself. I remember that morning well, as my mum and I were among the first in the queue and had such fun with the other people waiting. I did manage to get my bag and used it as it was intended, even though they were selling on the secondary market for stupid money at the time.

A designer whose impressive career has won her numerous accolades and, like me, an Essex girl born and bred, Anya Hindmarch is another powerhouse British name whose exceptional handbags just can't be ignored.

In 2009, Anya was both appointed Trustee of the Design Museum and awarded an MBE for her contribution to the British fashion industry.

'I'm very organised these days, and I keep my life in my handbag, like most women.'

Britt Ekland, actress

Chapter 11

Bags, Bags, Bags

I could write forever about the hundreds and thousands of wonderful handbags available today, but here I have covered most of the best-known contemporary designers, plus a few that you might not have heard of. There is so much choice out there now that it is near impossible for me to cover them all. Instead, I have focused on bags and designers that I personally have an affinity with and the ones that I truly believe are worth investing in as collectable pieces.

There are, of course, other fantastic designers out there. Michael Kors, Versace, Prada and Moschino, to name just a few, all produce stunning bag designs.

'I love Prada. Not so much the clothes, which are for malnourished thirteen-year-olds, but I covet, with covety covetousness, the shoes and handbags. Like, I LOVE them. If I was given a choice between world peace and a Prada handbag, I'd dither. (I'm not proud of this, I'm only saying.)'

Further Under the Duvet, Marian Keyes

Aside from those already mentioned, there are plenty of other bags that have captured my heart over the years. Helen Rochfort designed wonderful vintage-inspired bags that were handcrafted and released in small limited edition quantities with certificates of authenticity. My favourite, the *Willy Wonka* bag, smelled of chocolate.

Shoe and handbag designer Jimmy Choo released a limited edition clutch similar to the 1970s magazine bags. It featured the portrait *Nuclear* by the American photorealist artist Richard Phillips and is very difficult to come by now.

London-based milliner Phillip Treacy is renowned for his haute couture hat designs popular with celebrities and royalty. He has in the past, however, designed a range of handbags featuring iconic imagery by pop artist Andy Warhol. This featured box bag depicts Warhol's famous portrait of Elizabeth Taylor and is lined inside with Warhol's *Campbell's Soup Cans* print.

I have been fortunate over the decades to have owned some extremely rare and desirable handbags, as I am always on the lookout for that something special that screams future fashion collectable. For me, bags are not only about showcasing your personality or strutting proud as a peacock down the street with something over your arm that is admired by others. It is also about the artistry, as many bags are

The Helen Rochfort *Willy Wonka* bag smelled of chocolate.

works of art in their own right. I hunt out those that are different, bags that make a statement and have the potential to be investment pieces.

I admire the antique and vintage examples that not only transport us back in time but laid the foundations for the wonderful modern bags we have today. I am aware that modern bags will become sought after as vintage treasures in the future. I appreciate design, style and innovation. I get excited when I discover yet another bag that I wish to add to my collection. Handbags are far more than functional items for carrying necessities; they are an extension of who I am, they represent me as a person and they have become a part of my life, as every bag carries with it a meaning or a memory…

Handbags really can speak louder than words…

Andy Warhol Elizabeth Taylor box bag by Philip Treacy.

Tips for collecting and caring for your handbags

If you are considering starting your own handbag collection, be sure to keep the following tips in mind:

Always buy what you love. Use the bags you buy, take pleasure from them and then, if they increase in value you have invested wisely.

Don't feel you have to spend a fortune – only spend what you can afford. Start small and build up to the exciting designer bag that you have always dreamed of owning.

Seek out the quirkiest and most unusual designs – the more they resemble a work of art, the likelier they are to rise in value.

When buying high-end designer bags, always purchase from a reputable shop, dealer or through an auction house where specialist handbag experts are on hand to advise you on the bag you wish to buy. There are many counterfeit handbags on the market, sometimes being sold as genuine, so always check the authenticity. Ask for original receipts and any paperwork that comes with the bag. Most designer pieces also have serial numbers, so check for these too.

Always ask the seller about condition. Make sure there are no pen or makeup marks anywhere on exterior or interior of the bag. Always ensure the metal

Me with some of my prized handbags.

Lulu Guinness tote featuring a black cat on a red background.

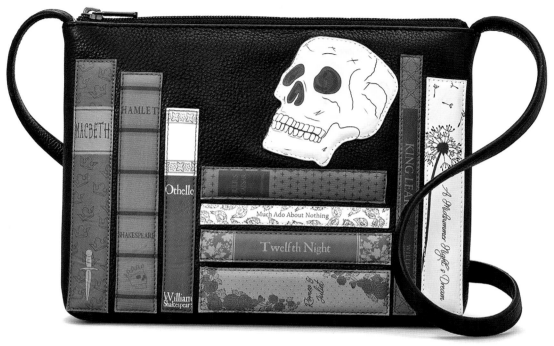

Yoshi *Bookworm Shakespeare* bag.

hardware is in good condition, there are no rips to the lining, the zips still work and that stitching is still intact.

Start small by hunting out bags from charity shops, boot sales and second hand dress agencies. You can unearth some real bargains, and this is a great place to start if you are entering the world of handbag collecting as a novice. I often pick up wonderful bags for very little money in places like this, and I always find it really exciting to be breathing new life into something that has been discarded by its previous owner.

Take care of your prized handbags. If they come with cloth dust bags, always keep them stored safely inside. Never place a handbag in a plastic covering as plastic is not breathable and can cause mould, ruining your handbag. When using a handbag, it's a good idea to place handbag liners inside it to protect it from spillages and any other accidental damage. This way, your prized possession will remain in excellent condition.

Never pile anything on top of your bags or throw them in the bottom of your wardrobe or under the bed, as they could end up out of shape or damaged.

When buying vintage bags condition is again paramount, although you need to take into account their age and previous use and understand that these bags may have slight flaws. It really depends on whether you are buying the handbag to use or

Me giving one of my lectures on vintage handbags.

purely as an investment. Collectors generally prefer mint condition where possible, as any form of damage can affect the value.

When buying hard bags such as those made of Lucite, plastic or wood, check for cracks, splits or shrinkage. This is especially important with Lucite bags as if they have been exposed to extreme heat they can shrink or warp, which can lead to loose lids and fittings. Always keep them away from sunlight and in a cool, dry environment.

Display your bags on shelves in cabinets, and always treat them like the treasured possessions that they are.

Index